The Anti-Inflammatory

COOKBOOK

for Beginners

Fast, Flavorful Meals to Boost Immunity and Restore Your Energy

Megan Sterling

FIX NOW:

The 5 Proven Secrets to an Inflammation-Free Life –
Transform Your Health, Diet, and Daily Habits for
Lasting Well-Being

Table of Contents

Introduction

The anti-inflammatory diet is gaining increasing recognition as a key to improving health and alleviating various health issues. This approach is based on the idea that certain foods can help reduce inflammation in the body, which in turn can decrease or even prevent a variety of health problems.

The anti-inflammatory diet plays a crucial role in managing a wide range of health concerns. Chronic inflammation is a common issue linked to many other diseases. It can lead to a variety of discomforts, including arthritis, a condition that causes joint inflammation, resulting in pain and limited mobility. Diabetes, a metabolic disorder characterized by high blood sugar levels, can also be influenced by inflammation, as it increases the risk of complications like nerve damage and heart disease.

Cardiovascular diseases are among the leading causes of morbidity and mortality worldwide, and chronic inflammation can contribute to their development by promoting atherosclerosis and other heart-related issues. Skin conditions like acne or eczema may also benefit from an anti-inflammatory diet, as inflammation often plays a role in these problems. By reducing inflammatory foods and incorporating anti-inflammatory ones, people dealing with these health issues might experience an improvement in their symptoms and overall quality of life.

This dietary approach not only aims to reduce inflammation but also to bring balance to the body and enhance overall well-being. It's important to understand that an anti-inflammatory diet is not just a short-term fix but a long-term lifestyle change that supports health in the long run. Therefore, it's essential to become familiar with the underlying principles of this diet and integrate them into daily life. This can be achieved by consuming fresh, unprocessed foods like fruits, vegetables, whole grains, healthy fats, and proteins. Additionally, staying well-hydrated is crucial to help the body flush out toxins and maintain proper hydration.

The anti-inflammatory diet can be viewed as a holistic approach to health promotion that not only addresses symptoms but also tackles the underlying causes of health issues. With a mindful dietary shift, many people can achieve an improved quality of life and long-term benefits from the positive effects of an anti-inflammatory diet.

Chapter 1

Inflammation

Inflammation is a vital defense mechanism of our body that plays a key role in fighting infections and healing injuries. When our body detects an injury, infection, or irritation, it initiates a complex process known as the inflammatory response. This response involves a series of biochemical and cellular changes designed to limit the harmful effects of the stimulus and begin the process of tissue repair.

Inflammation is often misunderstood as being purely harmful, but it is actually a crucial part of the body's healing toolkit. For example, when you cut or burn yourself, your body triggers an inflammatory response to protect the affected area, clean the wound, and promote the healing process. This reaction brings immune cells to the site of injury, which helps fight off any harmful bacteria or pathogens that might try to enter the body through the damaged skin. This type of inflammation, known as *acute inflammation*, is usually short-lived and resolves on its own once the injury or infection has healed.

In many cases, inflammation is a healthy and necessary reaction that helps the body recover from injuries and combat infections. Think of it as the body's internal emergency team, rushing to the site of injury or infection to ensure everything is under control. Swelling, redness, and pain in the affected area are signs that your body's natural defense mechanisms are hard at work. While these symptoms might feel uncomfortable, they are signs that your immune system is actively working to heal the body and restore balance.

However, inflammation can become a double-edged sword when it gets out of control. When the body's inflammatory response is overactive or lingers too long, it shifts from being a helpful process to one that can cause damage. This is known as *chronic inflammation*, and it can lead to a range of serious health problems. Unlike the short-term nature of acute inflammation, chronic inflammation is a slow-burning process that may persist for weeks, months, or even years, quietly damaging tissues and organs over time.

Acute Inflammation

Acute inflammation is a short-term, localized reaction that occurs when the body detects an injury or infection. It is a quick and efficient response aimed at minimizing damage and starting the healing process. This type of inflammation typically presents as redness, swelling, heat, and pain around the affected area. These symptoms are due to increased blood flow, which allows immune cells to reach the damaged tissue quickly.

For example, if you cut yourself while chopping vegetables, an acute inflammatory response kicks in immediately. The affected area may swell and feel warm as immune cells, like neutrophils and macrophages, rush to clean up damaged tissue and fend off any potential infections. The body repairs the wound, and the symptoms subside as healing progresses. This process is crucial for recovery and typically resolves on its own, allowing the body to return to normal.

Chronic Inflammation

In contrast, chronic inflammation is a long-term process that can persist even when there is no obvious injury or infection. While acute inflammation is a necessary part of healing, chronic inflammation can turn into a destructive force. It is often triggered by ongoing stress, a poor diet, lack of physical activity, environmental toxins, or autoimmune conditions where the immune system mistakenly attacks the body's own tissues.

When inflammation becomes chronic, it can lead to tissue damage and increase the risk of various illnesses. It has been linked to conditions such as cardiovascular disease, diabetes, cancer, rheumatoid arthritis, inflammatory bowel diseases like Crohn's and ulcerative colitis, and even mental health conditions like depression. The continuous presence of inflammatory markers in the body can disrupt normal cellular functions, leading to a wide range of complications.

What causes chronic inflammation?

The reasons are varied and can include an unhealthy diet, ongoing stress, lack of regular exercise, smoking, and exposure to environmental toxins. When these factors are present, they can trigger a low-grade inflammatory response that never quite shuts off. Over time, this ongoing inflammation can contribute to the development of serious health conditions such as heart disease, type 2 diabetes, cancer, arthritis, and neurodegenerative disorders like Alzheimer's disease.

The effects of chronic inflammation are far-reaching. It can silently attack the body's tissues, gradually weakening our defenses and making us more susceptible to illnesses. For example, chronic inflammation in the blood vessels can contribute to atherosclerosis, which increases the risk of heart attacks and strokes. Similarly, inflammation in the brain has been linked to cognitive decline and diseases like Alzheimer's. Addressing chronic inflammation isn't just about symptom relief—it's about preserving long-term health and vitality.

This makes managing inflammation a key part of maintaining overall health and preventing disease. Adopting an anti-inflammatory lifestyle, including regular exercise, a balanced diet, adequate sleep, and stress management, can go a long way in reducing chronic inflammation. An anti-inflammatory diet, in particular, is rich in foods like fresh fruits, vegetables, whole grains, healthy fats, and lean proteins, which help to reduce inflammation and support the body's natural healing processes.

Why Managing Inflammation is Essential

Understanding the difference between acute and chronic inflammation highlights the importance of keeping the inflammatory response balanced. The goal isn't to eliminate inflammation entirely—after all, we need it to fight infections and heal injuries. Instead, it's about keeping the process under control and preventing it from causing harm in the long run.

By focusing on the right foods and habits, you can help your body maintain a healthy inflammatory response. This means choosing a diet rich in anti-inflammatory foods, like berries, leafy greens, nuts, and omega-3-rich fish, while avoiding foods that are known to promote inflammation, such as processed sugars, refined carbs, and trans fats. Combining a mindful diet with regular physical activity, stress management techniques, and sufficient sleep creates a foundation for reducing chronic inflammation and improving overall health.

Chronic inflammation is a silent contributor to many serious health conditions. While acute inflammation is the body's natural way of healing, chronic inflammation lingers and can cause lasting damage. Here's how chronic inflammation is connected to various diseases:

Heart Disease

Chronic inflammation plays a significant role in heart disease by contributing to the buildup of plaque within the arteries, a condition known as atherosclerosis. This plaque hardens and narrows the arteries, making it difficult for blood to flow smoothly. As a result, the risk of blood clots, heart attacks, and strokes increases. Inflammation can also cause the plaque to become unstable, leading to sudden cardiovascular events.

Diabetes

Inflammation and insulin resistance go hand in hand. Chronic inflammation can disrupt the way cells respond to insulin, the hormone that helps regulate blood sugar levels. This resistance forces the pancreas to work harder to produce more insulin, eventually wearing it out. As insulin resistance worsens, the risk of developing Type 2 diabetes increases. For those already living with diabetes, chronic inflammation can exacerbate complications like nerve damage (diabetic neuropathy) and damage to blood vessels in the eyes (diabetic retinopathy).

Cancer

Chronic inflammation can create a favorable environment for the development and progression of certain cancers. Inflammation stimulates cell proliferation and survival, making it easier for abnormal cells to thrive and multiply. It can also cause DNA damage, which increases the risk of genetic mutations that can lead to cancer.

Furthermore, inflammatory cells release substances that can support the growth and spread of tumors, while also reducing the effectiveness of certain cancer treatments.

Arthritis

Chronic inflammation is central to various forms of arthritis, such as rheumatoid arthritis (RA) and osteoarthritis (OA). In RA, the immune system mistakenly attacks the joints, leading to persistent inflammation that causes joint pain, swelling, and deformities. In OA, long-term wear and tear can lead to inflammation that damages the cartilage, resulting in pain and stiffness. Both types of arthritis can significantly limit mobility and reduce the quality of life for those affected.

Neurodegenerative Diseases

The brain is particularly vulnerable to the damaging effects of chronic inflammation. Conditions like Alzheimer's and Parkinson's disease have been closely linked to prolonged inflammation in the brain. In Alzheimer's, inflammatory processes can accelerate the buildup of amyloid plaques, contributing to the death of nerve cells. In Parkinson's, chronic inflammation can damage the neurons that produce dopamine, a key neurotransmitter for movement. This contributes to the progression of symptoms such as memory loss, impaired thinking, and motor difficulties.

Gastrointestinal Issues

Chronic inflammation can wreak havoc on the digestive system, particularly in conditions like Crohn's disease and ulcerative colitis. These autoimmune diseases cause the immune system to attack the lining of the digestive tract, resulting in persistent inflammation, ulcers, and bleeding. The continuous irritation can disrupt nutrient absorption, leading to weight loss, fatigue, and other complications. Managing inflammation is crucial for reducing flare-ups and maintaining digestive health.

Skin Conditions

The skin, as the body's largest organ, can also suffer from chronic inflammation. Conditions like psoriasis, eczema, and acne often have an inflammatory component. In psoriasis, an overactive immune response leads to rapid skin cell turnover, resulting in scaly patches. Eczema causes itchy and inflamed skin, while acne involves inflammation in hair follicles. These conditions can cause physical discomfort and impact self-esteem, making inflammation management key to maintaining skin health.

Respiratory Diseases

Chronic inflammation in the respiratory system is a hallmark of conditions like asthma and chronic obstructive pulmonary disease (COPD). When inflammation persists in the airways, it leads to symptoms like coughing, wheezing, shortness of breath, and tightness in the chest. This ongoing irritation can make breathing difficult, affecting a person's ability to engage in everyday activities and diminishing their overall quality of life.

How to Manage Inflammation through Diet

Controlling inflammation starts with what you eat. Avoiding inflammation-promoting foods can help you manage and reduce your risk of the conditions mentioned above. Here are some of the biggest dietary offenders:

Sugar and Highly Processed Foods

Foods that are high in refined sugars and highly processed ingredients can have a detrimental impact on the body's inflammatory response, making them some of the primary culprits behind chronic inflammation. Consuming these foods leads to rapid spikes in blood sugar levels, which, in turn, can trigger a cascade of inflammatory reactions. The most common offenders include sugary sodas, candies, pastries, cookies, and various processed snacks that are staples in the modern diet.

When we consume high amounts of sugar, the body responds by releasing insulin to help regulate blood sugar levels. However, consistently high sugar intake can lead to insulin resistance—a condition in which the body's cells become less responsive to insulin. As a result, blood sugar levels remain elevated for longer periods, leading to chronic, low-grade inflammation. This prolonged inflammatory state has been linked to several health issues, including Type 2 diabetes, obesity, and cardiovascular diseases.

Moreover, the excessive consumption of sugar triggers the release of pro-inflammatory substances in the body, such as cytokines. These signaling molecules are intended to help the body respond to injury or infection, but when they are continuously activated by a high-sugar diet, they can contribute to a chronic inflammatory environment. This is especially problematic because the presence of these cytokines can exacerbate conditions like joint pain, metabolic syndrome, and autoimmune disorders.

Beyond sugars, many highly processed foods contain a variety of artificial additives, preservatives, and chemical compounds that can further amplify inflammation. Ingredients like high-fructose corn syrup, artificial sweeteners, flavor enhancers, and colorants are commonly found in processed snacks, packaged foods, and even so-called *health* drinks. These additives can irritate the gut lining, alter the balance of healthy bacteria in the digestive system, and stimulate the immune system to release inflammatory markers as a defense mechanism.

Processed foods also often contain unhealthy fats, such as trans fats and hydrogenated oils, which can further fuel inflammation. These fats are commonly found in fried foods, baked goods, margarine, and many packaged snacks, making it easy for them to sneak into our diet. Trans fats are known to increase the levels of LDL (bad) cholesterol while lowering HDL (good) cholesterol, leading to arterial inflammation and an increased risk of heart disease.

In addition, many processed products are loaded with excess sodium, which, when consumed in large quantities, can cause water retention and elevate blood pressure. High blood pressure is a known risk factor for heart disease and can contribute to vascular inflammation, further straining the cardiovascular system.

All these factors combined make sugar and highly processed foods a recipe for inflammation. While they may offer convenience and satisfy cravings in the short term, their long-term effects can be detrimental to health, contributing to the onset and progression of chronic diseases.

Trans Fats and Saturated Fats

Both trans fats and saturated fats can significantly contribute to inflammation, making them major dietary factors to consider when aiming to reduce chronic inflammation in the body. These fats are commonly found in everyday foods, yet their impact on our overall health can be profound, especially when consumed in large amounts.

Trans Fats: A Major Inflammatory Trigger

Trans fats are often found in fried foods, commercial baked goods, margarine, and a wide variety of processed snacks. These fats are created through a process called hydrogenation, which involves adding hydrogen to liquid vegetable oils to make them solid at room temperature. This process extends the shelf life of products but has serious health consequences.

When consumed, trans fats can raise levels of low-density lipoprotein (LDL) cholesterol—commonly known as *bad* cholesterol—while simultaneously lowering high-density lipoprotein (HDL) cholesterol, or *good* cholesterol. This imbalance contributes to the buildup of arterial plaque, which can lead to heart disease, high blood pressure, and strokes. But the risks don't stop at the cardiovascular system.

Trans fats have been shown to increase the production of pro-inflammatory cytokines, which are signaling proteins that direct the body's immune response. When cytokines are produced in excess, they can turn a healthy inflammatory response into a chronic condition, leading to damage in tissues and organs over time. This ongoing, low-grade inflammation is a contributing factor to conditions like diabetes, metabolic syndrome, and even certain types of cancer.

Additionally, trans fats can interfere with the body's natural ability to regulate inflammation. They inhibit the production of anti-inflammatory compounds like prostaglandins, which play a crucial role in controlling inflammation. As a result, the body is left in a constant state of heightened inflammatory response, making it more difficult to recover from injuries, fight infections, and maintain overall well-being.

Saturated Fats: A Delicate Balance

Saturated fats, found abundantly in animal products like red meat, butter, full-fat dairy, and some tropical oils like coconut and palm oil, are another type of fat that can exacerbate inflammation when consumed in excess. While saturated fats are not as harmful as trans fats, they still pose risks, particularly when they dominate the diet without balance from healthier fats.

One of the key ways saturated fats contribute to inflammation is by raising levels of LDL cholesterol. High levels of LDL cholesterol can lead to the accumulation of fatty deposits in the arteries, which is known as atherosclerosis. This condition causes the arterial walls to thicken and harden, making it more difficult for blood to flow and increasing the risk of cardiovascular events like heart attacks and strokes. The body's immune system perceives these fatty deposits as a threat, triggering an inflammatory response that can further damage arterial walls and exacerbate the condition.

Saturated fats can also influence the composition of the body's cellular membranes. When the diet is rich in saturated fats, the cell membranes become less flexible, which can impair the function of immune cells and make it harder for the body to respond effectively to inflammation. This change can negatively impact how the body processes other essential fats, like omega-3s, which are known for their anti-inflammatory properties.

While the body does need some saturated fats for hormone production and other physiological functions, balance is key. Consuming too much of these fats can tip the scales toward chronic inflammation, particularly when they replace healthier fats like those found in olive oil, avocados, nuts, and fatty fish.

Refined Carbohydrates

Refined carbohydrates are commonly found in foods like white bread, pastries, pasta, and many packaged snacks. While they may be convenient and often delicious, these carbs can wreak havoc on your body's inflammation levels. Refined carbs are made from grains that have been stripped of their bran and germ, the parts that contain fiber, vitamins, and minerals. What's left is a product that is quickly broken down into sugar by the body, leading to rapid spikes in blood glucose levels.

How Refined Carbs Impact Blood Sugar and Inflammation

When you consume refined carbohydrates, they cause a quick rise in blood sugar, prompting the body to release insulin to help process the sugar. This sudden surge can lead to a *sugar crash*, where blood glucose levels drop rapidly, creating a cycle of craving more high-carb foods. These constant spikes and drops in blood sugar levels can trigger an inflammatory response in the body, as the pancreas works overtime to manage insulin production. Over time, this can lead to insulin resistance, a condition where cells become less responsive to insulin, further promoting chronic inflammation and increasing the risk of Type 2 diabetes.

The Role of Fiber in Fighting Inflammation

One of the biggest differences between refined carbohydrates and their whole-grain counterparts is the presence of dietary fiber. Fiber is essential for maintaining stable blood sugar levels, as it slows the digestion process and prevents sudden sugar spikes. Whole grains like brown rice, quinoa, and whole-wheat products provide this crucial fiber, which not only supports blood sugar balance but also promotes gut health by feeding beneficial gut bacteria.

In contrast, refined carbs lack this fiber content, leading to faster digestion and absorption, which can result in a blood sugar roller coaster. The absence of fiber can also impair the balance of gut bacteria, contributing to what's known as *leaky gut syndrome*. This condition occurs when the lining of the digestive tract becomes more permeable, allowing harmful substances to enter the bloodstream and triggering an immune response. This chronic, low-grade inflammation in the gut can extend beyond the digestive system, impacting overall health and potentially leading to conditions like inflammatory bowel disease (IBD), Crohn's disease, and ulcerative colitis.

Refined Carbs and Systemic Inflammation

Beyond the digestive system, the inflammatory effects of refined carbohydrates can have a systemic impact on the body. The constant spikes in blood sugar can stimulate the release of pro-inflammatory substances like cytokines. These signaling proteins are part of the body's immune response, and when produced in excess, they can turn a beneficial immune reaction into chronic, widespread inflammation. This type of inflammation is associated with an increased risk of heart disease, obesity, metabolic syndrome, and even some forms of cancer.

Red Meat and Processed Meat

Excessive consumption of red meat, such as beef, lamb, and pork, as well as processed meats like sausages, bacon, hot dogs, and ham, has been strongly linked to an increased risk of chronic inflammatory conditions, including heart disease, certain cancers, and Type 2 diabetes. This connection is due to several factors inherent to these types of meats.

Firstly, red and processed meats are often high in saturated fats, which can raise levels of low-density lipoprotein (LDL) cholesterol, sometimes referred to as *bad* cholesterol. Elevated LDL levels are associated with an increase in systemic inflammation, which over time can contribute to the development of plaque in arteries, increasing the risk of atherosclerosis and cardiovascular disease.

Moreover, red meat contains a compound known as heme iron, which is found in animal products. While iron is an essential nutrient, excessive heme iron from red meat can lead to oxidative stress, promoting inflammation within the body. This oxidative stress can cause damage to cells, tissues, and DNA, potentially increasing the risk of conditions like colorectal cancer.

Processed meats present additional concerns due to the chemicals and preservatives used in their production. These products often contain nitrates and nitrites, which, when metabolized, can form nitrosamines—compounds that have been classified as carcinogenic. Furthermore, cooking meats at high temperatures, such as grilling, frying, or barbecuing, can produce heterocyclic amines (HCAs) and polycyclic aromatic hydrocarbons (PAHs), both of which are known to contribute to inflammation and increase cancer risk.

The high salt content in processed meats also poses a problem. Sodium-rich diets can cause water retention and raise blood pressure, both of which can lead to inflammation. This combination of saturated fats, heme iron, chemical additives, and sodium creates a perfect storm that can fuel inflammatory processes in the body, making it important to be mindful of the amount and type of meat consumed.

Anti-Inflammatory Diet for Better Health

The good news is that by adopting an anti-inflammatory diet, you can counteract the harmful effects of these pro-inflammatory foods. Embracing a diet that prioritizes whole, plant-based foods like colorful fruits and vegetables, whole grains, nuts, seeds, and healthy fats such as those found in olive oil and avocados can significantly reduce inflammation. Lean proteins like fish, poultry, and plant-based sources such as legumes and tofu can replace red and processed meats, offering a more heart-friendly source of protein.

This dietary shift not only helps reduce the body's inflammatory response but also supports long-term health and vitality. In the following chapters, we will take a deeper dive into the principles of an anti-inflammatory diet, providing you with practical guidance on how to make these dietary changes. You'll also find a wide variety of delicious, easy-to-follow recipes that will make it easy to incorporate these foods into your daily routine. With these tools at your disposal, you can embark on a journey toward a healthier, more vibrant life, free from the discomforts of chronic inflammation.

Chapter 2

How Does the Anti-Inflammatory Diet Work?

The anti-inflammatory diet is based on the different properties of foods, which can either promote or reduce inflammation in the body. Inflammation-promoting foods, such as refined sugar, processed foods, trans fats, and saturated fats, can increase inflammation within the body. These foods activate inflammatory processes that can lead to a variety of health problems, including heart disease, diabetes, and cancer. By impacting blood sugar levels and triggering the release of pro-inflammatory cytokines, these foods encourage a chronic inflammatory response in the body.

On the other hand, anti-inflammatory foods help reduce inflammation and promote overall health. Key anti-inflammatory foods include those rich in omega-3 fatty acids, such as salmon, mackerel, and flaxseeds. Omega-3 fatty acids are well-known for their anti-inflammatory properties and can help reduce inflammation in the body by inhibiting the production of pro-inflammatory cytokines.

Antioxidant-rich foods like berries, leafy greens, turmeric, and ginger also have anti-inflammatory effects. These foods contain antioxidants that neutralize free radicals, helping to combat inflammation. Additionally, fiber-rich foods such as whole grains, legumes, and vegetables can contribute to reducing inflammation in the body. Fiber supports digestion and promotes a healthy gut flora, which in turn can help lower inflammation.

The goal of the anti-inflammatory diet is to balance inflammatory and anti-inflammatory foods to control the body's inflammatory response and reduce chronic inflammation. By adopting an anti-inflammatory diet, people can improve their health and lower their risk of various diseases. It's important to view this diet as part of a long-term lifestyle that includes regular exercise, adequate sleep, and stress management for optimal results. Ultimately, the anti-inflammatory diet can be seen as a holistic approach to promoting health and well-being, emphasizing the importance of a balanced diet and a healthy lifestyle

The Power of Anti-Inflammatory Foods

Choosing the right foods plays a crucial role in combating inflammation in the body. This section highlights the most important anti-inflammatory foods that can help reduce inflammation and promote health. By incorporating these foods into your daily diet, you can achieve an anti-inflammatory effect that leads to improved well-being over time. Here are some of the most effective anti-inflammatory foods that you can easily incorporate into your diet.

Salmon

Salmon is a powerhouse when it comes to anti-inflammatory nutrition, thanks to its high levels of omega-3 fatty acids, particularly EPA and DHA. These essential fats work to reduce the production of inflammatory molecules in the body, helping to protect against chronic conditions like heart disease and arthritis. Regular consumption of salmon can support joint health and improve cardiovascular function, making it a staple of any anti-inflammatory diet.

Blueberries

Rich in antioxidants like anthocyanins and vitamin C, blueberries are excellent for combating inflammation. These antioxidants help neutralize free radicals—unstable molecules that can damage cells and promote inflammation. Blueberries can help protect against oxidative stress, which is linked to chronic inflammation, aging, and the onset of various diseases.

Spinach

Spinach is packed with vitamin E, a key nutrient in reducing inflammation. Vitamin E can inhibit the activity of proteins in the body that promote inflammation, helping to manage symptoms of conditions like asthma and arthritis. Spinach is also rich in other nutrients, like magnesium and iron, making it a versatile addition to your meals.

Turmeric

Known for its vibrant yellow color, turmeric is one of the most potent anti-inflammatory spices. Its active compound, curcumin, has been shown to inhibit inflammatory enzymes and reduce the production of signaling molecules that trigger inflammation. Turmeric's benefits extend beyond inflammation, offering support for digestive health and joint mobility as well.

Ginger

Ginger, a warming spice, contains gingerol—a bioactive compound with powerful anti-inflammatory effects. Gingerol can reduce the release of inflammatory molecules, making it effective in managing symptoms like joint pain and muscle soreness. Incorporating fresh or powdered ginger into your diet can also support digestion and help soothe an upset stomach.

Walnuts

Walnuts are rich in omega-3 fatty acids and vitamin E, both of which have been shown to help reduce inflammation. These nutrients work by lowering levels of inflammatory markers in the blood, such as C-reactive protein. Adding a handful of walnuts to your daily diet can support heart health and improve overall inflammation levels.

Extra Virgin Olive Oil

A key ingredient in the Mediterranean diet, extra virgin olive oil is known for its anti-inflammatory properties, particularly due to a compound called oleocanthal. Oleocanthal functions similarly to non-steroidal anti-inflammatory drugs (NSAIDs) by inhibiting the production of inflammatory molecules. Using olive oil in place of other fats can help reduce inflammation and support a healthy heart.

Berries (Strawberries, Raspberries, Blackberries)

These berries are rich in antioxidants like anthocyanins, which help inhibit inflammation-promoting enzymes in the body. The high levels of vitamin C in these fruits also support immune function and skin health, making them a delicious way to combat inflammation while satisfying your sweet tooth.

Kale

Kale is a nutrient-dense leafy green that contains vitamin E and beta-carotene, both of which have potent anti-inflammatory effects. These nutrients help reduce the production of molecules that promote inflammation, supporting a balanced immune response. Kale is also an excellent source of fiber, which is essential for maintaining gut health.

Chia Seeds

These tiny seeds are a nutritional powerhouse, rich in omega-3 fatty acids and fiber. Omega-3s help reduce inflammation in the body, while the fiber in chia seeds supports a healthy gut microbiome, which plays a crucial role in regulating immune function and inflammation. Adding chia seeds to smoothies, yogurt, or oatmeal is an easy way to enhance your anti-inflammatory diet.

Cinnamon

Cinnamon is more than just a warming spice—it contains anti-inflammatory compounds like cinnamaldehyde, which can help reduce inflammation in the body. The antioxidants in cinnamon, such as polyphenols, also protect against oxidative stress. Cinnamon can be a comforting addition to both sweet and savory dishes, providing flavor and health benefits.

Avocado

Avocados are a rich source of vitamin E and carotenoids, like lutein and zeaxanthin, which help reduce inflammation. These nutrients support healthy skin, vision, and immune function, making avocados a valuable addition to any anti-inflammatory meal plan. Their healthy fats also make them satisfying, helping to keep you full and energized.

Garlic

Garlic contains allicin, a sulfur compound with potent anti-inflammatory properties. Allicin can reduce the production of inflammatory cytokines, helping to alleviate symptoms of conditions like arthritis. Garlic is also known for its immune-boosting properties, making it a flavorful way to protect your body from illness.

Sweet Potatoes

High in beta-carotene, sweet potatoes offer anti-inflammatory benefits by helping to regulate the body's immune response. Beta-carotene is converted into vitamin A in the body, which is crucial for maintaining healthy mucous membranes and reducing inflammation in the respiratory system. Sweet potatoes also provide a healthy source of carbohydrates and fiber.

Celery

Celery is a low-calorie vegetable with powerful anti-inflammatory compounds like apigenin and luteolin. These compounds work to suppress the activity of inflammatory enzymes, helping to reduce inflammation throughout the body. Celery's high water content also makes it a great choice for hydration and digestion.

Pomegranate Seeds

Rich in polyphenols like ellagic acid, pomegranate seeds can combat inflammation by neutralizing free radicals and reducing oxidative stress. These antioxidants are known to inhibit enzymes that promote inflammation, making pomegranates a powerful addition to your diet for heart and joint health.

Broccoli

Broccoli contains sulforaphane, a compound with potent anti-inflammatory effects that can help regulate the body's response to inflammation. Sulforaphane supports liver detoxification and helps eliminate toxins that can contribute to inflammation. Adding broccoli to your diet can promote a healthy immune system and support overall wellness.

Beets

Beets are rich in betalains and betaine, which are known for their ability to reduce inflammation. These compounds help to inhibit enzymes that promote inflammation and protect cells from damage. Beets also support healthy blood flow, making them an excellent choice for cardiovascular health.

Balancing Inflammation for Better Health

The anti-inflammatory diet isn't about restrictive eating or counting every calorie; it's about making mindful choices that promote a balanced and sustainable approach to health. Instead of focusing on what you *can't* eat, it encourages you to prioritize whole, nutrient-dense foods that naturally reduce inflammation, such as fresh vegetables, antioxidant-rich fruits, healthy fats, and lean proteins. These foods work in harmony with your body, supporting its natural healing processes, reducing oxidative stress, and combating chronic inflammation that can contribute to conditions like heart disease, diabetes, and autoimmune disorders.

By choosing anti-inflammatory foods over those that promote inflammation, you can create a diet that not only prevents illness but also boosts your energy, supports digestion, and improves overall vitality. It's a lifestyle change that's achievable for everyone, and it doesn't require sacrificing flavor or enjoyment.

In the following chapters, you'll find practical ways to incorporate these powerful, inflammation-fighting ingredients into your daily meals. From vibrant breakfast bowls that kickstart your day with energy to satisfying lunches, hearty dinners, and even indulgent desserts, this guide will show you that eating for health can be both delicious and fulfilling. Each recipe is crafted to satisfy your taste buds while supporting your body's needs, making it easier than ever to adopt this nourishing way of eating. Get ready to embrace a lifestyle that fuels your body with everything it needs to thrive—one delicious bite at a time.

Chapter 3
Breakfast Ideas

Welcome to the third chapter of our anti-inflammatory diet guide: *Breakfast Ideas*. Breakfast is more than just the first meal of the day—it's an opportunity to fuel your body with the right nutrients that can set a positive tone for the hours ahead. A well-balanced breakfast provides the energy you need to stay focused, boosts your metabolism, and keeps inflammation in check from the moment you wake up.

In this chapter, we'll introduce you to a variety of creative and nourishing breakfast options that are not only anti-inflammatory but also delicious and easy to prepare. From hearty oatmeal bowls topped with antioxidant-rich berries and crunchy nuts to creamy avocado scrambled eggs on whole-grain toast, and vibrant green smoothies infused with ginger and turmeric—these recipes are designed to delight your taste buds and kickstart your morning with a healthy boost. Enjoy these breakfast ideas, and feel the difference as they energize your mornings and support your journey towards a balanced, inflammation-free life.

Peanut Butter Banana Sandwich with Chia Seeds

 5 Min   0 Min    4

This quick and delicious peanut butter banana sandwich is perfect for a nutritious breakfast or snack. The chia seeds add a crunchy texture and extra fiber, making this simple sandwich both satisfying and healthy.

Ingredients:

✧ 8 slices whole-grain bread
✧ 4 tablespoons peanut butter
✧ 4 ripe bananas, sliced
✧ 4 tablespoons chia seeds

Directions:

✧ Lay out the slices of whole-grain bread on a clean surface.
✧ Spread 1 tablespoon of peanut butter evenly on each slice.
✧ Arrange the banana slices on top of the peanut butter on four of the slices.
✧ Sprinkle 1 tablespoon of chia seeds over the bananas on each sandwich.
✧ Place the remaining slices of bread on top to complete the sandwiches.
✧ Cut the sandwiches in half if desired, and serve immediately.

Nutritional Information per Serving - Calories: 300 Fat: 20 g Sodium: 250 mg Carbohydrates: 25 g Protein: 7 g Fiber: 5 g

Mixed Berry Chia Pudding with Almonds

 10 Min* 0 Min 4

* Plus 2 hours of overnight chilling

This creamy chia pudding, packed with the goodness of mixed berries and crunchy almonds, makes for a delicious and nutritious start to your day. It's perfect for meal prep, as it can be made ahead of time and customized with your favorite toppings.

Ingredients:

✧ 1/2 cup chia seeds
✧ 2 cups almond milk (or another plant-based milk)
✧ 2 cups mixed berries (fresh or frozen)
✧ 1/4 cup chopped almonds (for garnish)
✧ Honey or maple syrup (optional, for sweetening)

Directions:

✧ In a large bowl, mix the chia seeds with the almond milk, stirring well to ensure the seeds are fully immersed in the liquid.
✧ Cover the bowl and refrigerate for at least 2 hours or overnight until the mixture reaches a pudding-like consistency.
✧ Once ready, give the chia pudding a good stir to ensure even texture.
✧ Divide the pudding evenly into four bowls or glasses.
✧ Top each serving with mixed berries and a sprinkle of chopped almonds.
✧ Drizzle with honey or maple syrup if desired.
✧ Serve immediately or keep refrigerated until ready to enjoy.

Nutritional Information per Serving - Calories: 250 Fat: 15 g Sodium: 70 mg Carbohydrates: 20 g Protein: 7 g Fiber: 12 g

Ingredients:

✧ 4 handfuls of fresh spinach leaves
✧ 4 ripe bananas
✧ 2 green apples, cored and roughly chopped
✧ 1-inch piece of ginger, peeled and chopped
✧ 2 cups water or coconut water
✧ Juice of 2 lemons
✧ Optional: ice cubes for cooling

Green Spinach and Ginger Smoothie

 5 Min  0 Min 4

Kickstart your day with this refreshing and nutrient-packed green smoothie. The combination of spinach, banana, and ginger creates a perfect blend of flavors, while the ginger adds a zesty kick. This smoothie is great for boosting your energy levels and providing essential vitamins and minerals.

Directions:

✧ Thoroughly wash the fresh spinach leaves. Peel the bananas and chop them into chunks. Core and roughly chop the green apples.
✧ Place the spinach, banana pieces, apple chunks, and chopped ginger into a blender.
✧ Add the water or coconut water and squeeze in the juice of two lemons. Optionally, add ice cubes to chill the smoothie and adjust the consistency.
✧ Blend all the ingredients until smooth. Pour the green smoothie into glasses and serve immediately.

Nutritional Information per Serving - Calories: 120 Fat: 1 g Sodium: 10 mg Carbohydrates: 30 g Protein: 2 g Fiber: 5 g

Avocado Toast with Tomatoes and Arugula

 10 Min   5 Min   4

Ingredients:

- 4 ripe avocados
- 4 slices whole-grain bread
- 4 tomatoes, sliced
- 1 cup arugula
- Salt and pepper to taste
- Optional: lemon juice or balsamic vinegar for drizzling

This classic avocado toast gets a flavorful upgrade with juicy tomatoes and peppery arugula. It's a quick, nutritious breakfast or snack that's rich in healthy fats and vitamins. For a zesty kick, drizzle with lemon juice or balsamic vinegar.

Directions:

- Halve the avocados, remove the pits, and scoop out the flesh into a bowl.
- Mash the avocado with a fork and season with salt and pepper.
- Toast the slices of whole-grain bread until they are crispy.
- Generously spread the mashed avocado over each slice of toasted bread.
- Top with tomato slices, then evenly distribute the arugula over the tomatoes.
- Drizzle with lemon juice or balsamic vinegar if desired.
- Serve the avocado toast immediately and enjoy!

Nutritional Information per Serving - Calories: 300 Fat: 20 g Sodium: 400 mg Carbohydrates: 25 g Protein: 7 g Fiber: 5 g

Quinoa Breakfast Bowl with Berries

 15 Min*   0 Min  4

* Plus quinoa cooking time

Ingredients:

- 1 cup quinoa
- 2 cups water
- 1 cup mixed berries (e.g., strawberries, raspberries, blueberries)
- 4 tablespoons chopped almonds or walnuts
- 4 teaspoons honey or maple syrup (optional, for sweetening)
- A pinch of cinnamon (optional)

This hearty and nutritious quinoa bowl is the perfect way to start your day. Packed with protein, fiber, and antioxidants, it's a delicious and satisfying breakfast that will keep you energized. Feel free to customize it with your favorite nuts or a sprinkle of cinnamon.

Directions:

- Rinse the quinoa thoroughly under running water to remove any bitterness.
- Combine the rinsed quinoa with 2 cups of water in a medium saucepan and bring to a boil.
- Reduce the heat and let the quinoa simmer for about 12-15 minutes, until the water is fully absorbed, and the quinoa is tender.
- Transfer the cooked quinoa into four bowls and let it cool slightly.
- Top each bowl with mixed berries and a tablespoon of chopped nuts. Drizzle with a teaspoon of honey or maple syrup if desired, and optionally sprinkle a pinch of cinnamon on top.
- Serve the quinoa breakfast bowl immediately and enjoy!

Nutritional Information per Serving - Calories: 250 Fat: 5 g Sodium: 10 mg Carbohydrates: 45 g Protein: 8 g Fiber: g 6

Coconut Yogurt with Pomegranate and Walnuts

 5 Min   0 Min   4

This simple yet flavorful coconut yogurt bowl is topped with juicy pomegranate seeds and crunchy walnuts. It's a perfect quick breakfast or snack that's both satisfying and nutritious. For added sweetness, a drizzle of honey or maple syrup works wonderfully.

Ingredients:

- ✧ 2 cups coconut yogurt
- ✧ 2 pomegranates, seeds removed
- ✧ 1/2 cup walnuts, roughly chopped
- ✧ Optional: 4 teaspoons honey or maple syrup (for sweetening)

Directions:

- ✧ Divide the coconut yogurt evenly into four bowls.
- ✧ Halve the pomegranates and remove the seeds, then sprinkle them over the yogurt.
- ✧ Top each bowl with a generous amount of chopped walnuts.
- ✧ If desired, drizzle with a teaspoon of honey or maple syrup for added sweetness.
- ✧ Serve immediately and enjoy this refreshing and nutritious treat!

Nutritional Information per Serving - Calories: 200 Fat: 20 g Sodium: 15 mg Carbohydrates: 30 g Protein: 7 g Fiber: 5 g

Oatmeal Pancakes with Blueberries

Ingredients:

- ✧ 1/2 cup oats
- ✧ 1 ripe banana
- ✧ 1 large egg
- ✧ 1/2 cup fresh blueberries
- ✧ A pinch of cinnamon
- ✧ 1 tablespoon coconut oil or butter for cooking

 15 Min  0 Min   4

These hearty oatmeal pancakes are packed with fiber and natural sweetness from bananas. They make for a perfect weekend breakfast and can be topped with fresh blueberries for an extra burst of flavor. Try them with a drizzle of maple syrup for added indulgence.

Directions:

- ✧ Place the oats in a bowl and cover them with hot water.
- ✧ Let them soak for about 5 minutes until softened.
- ✧ In a separate bowl, mash the banana with a fork, then add the egg and mix well.
- ✧ Stir the soaked oats into the banana-egg mixture, ensuring everything is well combined. Add a pinch of cinnamon and stir again.
- ✧ Heat a skillet over medium heat and melt the coconut oil or butter.
- ✧ Pour a ladle of batter into the skillet, spreading it out to form small pancakes. Cook the pancakes for about 2-3 minutes on each side until golden brown and cooked through.
- ✧ Serve the oatmeal pancakes topped with fresh blueberries and enjoy them warm.

Nutritional Information per Serving - Calories: 350 Fat: 10 g Sodium: 75 mg Carbohydrates: 50 g Protein: 10 g Fiber: 7 g

Fruity Acai Bowl with Honey and Almonds

 10 Min   0 Min   4

This vibrant acai bowl is a refreshing and nutritious way to start your day. Packed with antioxidants and topped with crunchy almonds, it's as delicious as it is healthy. Customize it with your favorite fresh berries for added flavor and texture.

Ingredients:

- ✧ 7 oz frozen acai berry puree (about 2 packets)
- ✧ 2 ripe bananas, sliced
- ✧ 2 cups frozen mixed berries (e.g., strawberries, raspberries, blueberries)
- ✧ 4 tablespoons honey
- ✧ 1/4 cup almonds, chopped
- ✧ A handful of fresh berries for garnish

Directions:

- ✧ In a blender, combine the frozen acai berry puree, sliced bananas, and frozen mixed berries.
- ✧ Add the honey and blend until you achieve a smooth, creamy consistency.
- ✧ Pour the acai mixture into four bowls, smoothing the tops with a spoon.
- ✧ Sprinkle each bowl with chopped almonds and garnish with fresh berries.
- ✧ Serve immediately and enjoy this deliciously fruity breakfast bowl!

Nutritional Information per Serving - Calories: 300 Fat: 10 g Sodium: 20 mg Carbohydrates: 45 g Protein: 5 g Fiber: 8 g

Sweet Potato Hash Browns with Avocado and Egg

 20 Min   0 Min   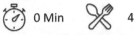 4

Ingredients:

- ✧ 4 medium sweet potatoes
- ✧ 4 ripe avocados
- ✧ 4 large eggs
- ✧ Salt and pepper to taste
- ✧ 4 tablespoons olive oil or coconut oil for frying
- ✧ Fresh cilantro or parsley for garnish (optional)

These crispy sweet potato hash browns are topped with creamy avocado and a perfectly fried egg, making for a delicious and satisfying breakfast. Garnish with fresh herbs for an extra burst of flavor.

Directions:

- ✧ Peel the sweet potatoes and grate them coarsely.
- ✧ Place the grated sweet potatoes in a clean kitchen towel and squeeze out any excess moisture.
- ✧ Transfer the sweet potatoes to a bowl, seasoning with salt and pepper.
- ✧ Heat a skillet over medium heat and add a tablespoon of olive oil or coconut oil. Place a portion of the seasoned sweet potatoes in the skillet, flattening it into a hash brown shape. Cook for about 5-7 minutes on each side, until golden brown and crispy.
- ✧ While the hash browns are cooking, halve the avocados, remove the pits, and scoop out the flesh. Slice or mash the avocado according to your preference.
- ✧ In a separate pan, fry the eggs until the whites are set, but the yolks remain slightly runny.
- ✧ To serve, place each sweet potato hash brown on a plate, top with avocado slices or mash, and place the fried egg on top. Garnish with fresh cilantro or parsley if desired.
- ✧ Serve immediately and enjoy!

Nutritional Information per Serving - Calories: 350 Fat: 20 g Sodium: 120 mg Carbohydrates: 45 g Protein: 10 g Fiber: 8 g

Matcha Chia Pudding with Mango

 5 Min*   0 Min ⚔ 4

* Plus chilling time

This refreshing matcha chia pudding is a perfect blend of creamy texture and tropical sweetness. The addition of mango adds a vibrant, fruity flavor, making it an ideal breakfast or snack option. Customize with a drizzle of honey or maple syrup if you like it sweeter.

Ingredients:

✧ 1/2 cup chia seeds
✧ 2 teaspoons matcha powder
✧ 2 cups almond milk or other plant-based milk
✧ 2 ripe mangoes, diced
✧ Optional: honey or maple syrup for sweetening

Directions:

✧ In a medium bowl, combine the chia seeds and matcha powder.
✧ Add the almond milk and stir well to ensure there are no lumps.
✧ Cover the mixture and refrigerate for at least 2 hours or overnight until the chia seeds have absorbed the liquid and the pudding has set.
✧ Once the chia pudding is ready, stir it to achieve a smooth consistency. Divide the pudding evenly among four bowls and top each with diced mango.
✧ If desired, drizzle with honey or maple syrup for added sweetness.
✧ Serve and enjoy this deliciously nutritious treat!

Nutritional Information per Serving - Calories: 250 Fat: 10 g Sodium: 60 mg Carbohydrates: 35 g Protein: 5 g Fiber: 10 g

Whole Grain Sandwich with Smoked Salmon, Avocado, and Radishes

Ingredients:

✧ 8 slices whole grain bread
✧ 7 oz smoked salmon
✧ 2 ripe avocados, sliced
✧ 4 radishes, thinly sliced
✧ Fresh cress or chives for garnish
✧ Salt and pepper to taste
✧ Optional: lemon wedges for drizzling

 10 Min  0 Min 4

This nutritious whole grain sandwich is layered with creamy avocado, smoked salmon, and crisp radishes, making it a perfect option for a quick, healthy lunch. Add a squeeze of lemon for a refreshing tang, and garnish with fresh herbs for extra flavor.

Directions:

✧ Lightly toast the whole grain bread slices if desired.
✧ Layer the smoked salmon evenly over four slices of the bread.
✧ Arrange the avocado slices on top of the salmon, followed by a scattering of radish slices.
✧ Season with salt and pepper to taste, then garnish with fresh cress or chives.
✧ Place the remaining bread slices on top to complete the sandwiches.
✧ If desired, drizzle with a little lemon juice for extra flavor.
✧ Serve immediately and enjoy this satisfying and nutritious meal!

Nutritional Information per Serving - Calories: 350 Fat: 20 g Sodium: 500 mg Carbohydrates: 25 g Protein: 15 g Fiber: 8 g

Beetroot Smoothie with Orange and Ginger

 10 Min   0 Min   4

This vibrant beetroot smoothie is a refreshing and nutrient-packed blend that combines the earthiness of beets with the zesty kick of ginger and the sweetness of orange. It's perfect for a morning boost or a post-workout treat.

Ingredients:

✧ 1 small beet, cooked and peeled
✧ Juice of 4 oranges
✧ 4 teaspoons freshly grated ginger
✧ 4 ripe bananas
✧ 4 handfuls of spinach leaves
✧ Optional: a few ice cubes

Directions:

✧ Cut the cooked and peeled beet into chunks.
✧ Squeeze the juice from the oranges.
✧ In a blender, combine the beet pieces, orange juice, freshly grated ginger, ripe bananas, and spinach leaves.
✧ If you prefer a cooler and slightly thinner smoothie, add a few ice cubes.
✧ Blend all the ingredients until smooth.
✧ Pour the beetroot smoothie into glasses and serve immediately.

Nutritional Information per Serving - Calories: 20' Fat: 1 g Sodium: 35 mg Carbohydrates: 45 g Protein: 4 g Fiber: 8 g

Ingredients:

✧ 1 cup quinoa
✧ 1 cup water
✧ 1 cup almond milk or other plant-based milk
✧ 2 small apples, peeled and diced
✧ 4 teaspoons cinnamon
✧ 4 tablespoons maple syrup or honey (optional for sweetening)
✧ A pinch of salt
✧ A handful of chopped walnuts or almonds for garnish

Quinoa Porridge with Apples and Cinnamon

 15 Min   0 Min   4

This warm and comforting quinoa porridge is a delightful way to start your day. The combination of apples and cinnamon creates a cozy flavor, while quinoa provides a hearty, protein-packed base. Top with nuts for a satisfying crunch.

Directions:

✧ Rinse the quinoa thoroughly under running water to remove any bitterness.
✧ Combine the rinsed quinoa with the water in a small saucepan and bring to a boil.
✧ Reduce the heat and simmer for about 12-15 minutes, until the water is fully absorbed and the quinoa is tender.
✧ While the quinoa is cooking, heat the almond milk in a separate pot.
✧ Once the quinoa is cooked, mix it with the warm almond milk. Stir in the diced apples and cinnamon, combining everything well.
✧ Sweeten with maple syrup or honey if desired. Serve the quinoa porridge in bowls and garnish with chopped walnuts or almonds.
✧ Enjoy immediately!

Nutritional Information per Serving - Calories: 300 Fat: 10 g Sodium: 40 mg Carbohydrates: 45 g Protein: 8 g Fiber: 6 g

Chapter 4

Healthy Snacks and Appetizers

This chapter offers a variety of delicious options for light meals, snacks, or appetizers that not only satisfy your hunger but also nourish your body with essential nutrients. Whether you're looking for a quick bite between meals or healthy options to serve at gatherings, this chapter has you covered with a range of flavorful choices. In this chapter, you'll find creative recipes that are easy to prepare, healthy, and well-balanced. From refreshing salads and crunchy veggie sticks with creamy dips to protein-rich snacks like spiced nuts and energy bites, there's something to suit every taste. These recipes are perfect for midday snacks, party nibbles, or as a tasty start to your meals, helping you stay on track with your health goals without sacrificing flavor. Explore the range of healthy and satisfying options that will elevate your snack and appetizer game. Let these simple yet delicious recipes inspire you to support your healthy lifestyle while treating your taste buds and keeping inflammation at bay.

Hummus Dip with Fresh Veggie Sticks

Ingredients:

✧ 7 oz canned chickpeas, drained
✧ 4 tablespoons tahini (sesame paste)
✧ 2 garlic cloves, chopped
✧ 4 tablespoons lemon juice
✧ 4 tablespoons olive oil
✧ A pinch of salt and pepper
✧ Assorted veggie sticks (e.g., carrots, celery, cucumbers, bell peppers)

 10 Min 0 Min ✗ 4

This creamy hummus dip is paired with fresh, crunchy veggie sticks for a healthy and satisfying snack. It's perfect for parties, picnics, or just a quick snack at home.

Directions:

✧ In a blender or food processor, combine the drained chickpeas, tahini, chopped garlic, lemon juice, olive oil, salt, and pepper.
✧ Blend until smooth and creamy, adding a little water if needed to reach your desired consistency.
✧ Transfer the hummus to a serving bowl and serve with an assortment of fresh veggie sticks.
✧ Enjoy immediately!

Nutritional Information per Serving - Calories: 180 Fat: 10 g Sodium: 120 mg Carbohydrates: 15 g Protein: 6 g Fiber: g 5

Avocado Hummus Dip

 10 Min   0 Min   ✕ 4

Ingredients:

✧ 1 ripe avocado
✧ 1 can (15 oz) chickpeas, drained and rinsed
✧ 2 garlic cloves, chopped
✧ Juice of 1 lemon
✧ 2 tablespoons olive oil
✧ Salt and pepper to taste
✧ A pinch of ground cumin
✧ Fresh vegetables for serving (e.g., carrot sticks, cucumber slices, bell pepper strips)

This creamy avocado hummus dip combines the richness of avocado with the classic flavors of hummus, creating a delicious and healthy snack. Perfect for dipping fresh veggies, it's a great option for parties or a light snack.

Directions:

✧ Halve the avocado, remove the pit, and scoop out the flesh.
✧ In a blender or food processor, combine the chickpeas, chopped garlic, lemon juice, olive oil, salt, pepper, and cumin.
✧ Add the avocado and blend until smooth and creamy.
✧ Transfer the avocado hummus dip to a bowl and serve with fresh vegetable sticks.

Nutritional Information per Serving - Calories: 450' Fat: 15 g Sodium: 250 mg Carbohydrates: 45 g Protein: 7 g Fiber: 8 g

Quinoa Salad with Roasted Vegetables and Lemon Dressing

 15 Min   20 Min   ✕ 4

This vibrant quinoa salad is packed with roasted vegetables and topped with a zesty lemon dressing. It's a perfect light meal or side dish that's both nutritious and flavorful. Add a handful of arugula for extra freshness and a sprinkle of toasted pine nuts for a satisfying crunch.

Directions:

✧ Rinse the quinoa to remove bitterness, then cook with water or vegetable broth for 15 minutes until tender.
✧ Preheat the oven to 400°F and roast sliced bell pepper, zucchini, and carrots with olive oil, salt, and pepper for 15-20 minutes.
✧ Prepare a lemon dressing by whisking the ingredients together. In a large bowl, combine cooled quinoa, roasted vegetables, arugula, and parsley.
✧ Toss with the lemon dressing and top with toasted pine nuts before serving.

Ingredients:

✧ 1 cup quinoa
✧ 2 cups water or vegetable broth
✧ 1 small red bell pepper, sliced
✧ 1 small zucchini, sliced
✧ 1 small carrot, thinly sliced
✧ 1 tablespoon olive oil
✧ Salt and pepper to taste
✧ A handful of fresh arugula leaves
✧ 1 tablespoon chopped fresh parsley
✧ 1 tablespoon toasted pine nuts
✧ Juice of 1 lemon
✧ 1 tablespoon olive oil
✧ 1 teaspoon honey or maple syrup
✧ A pinch of salt and pepper

Nutritional Information per Serving - Calories: 350 Fat: 10 g Sodium: 250 mg Carbohydrates: 45 g Protein: 8 g Fiber: 8 g

Rosemary Sweet Potato Fries with Avocado Dip

 10 Min 25 Min  4

These crispy rosemary-infused sweet potato fries are the perfect healthy alternative to regular fries. Paired with a creamy avocado dip, they make a delicious snack or side dish that's full of flavor and nutrition.

Ingredients:

- ✧ 2 medium sweet potatoes
- ✧ 2 tablespoons olive oil
- ✧ 2 teaspoons fresh or dried rosemary leaves
- ✧ Salt and pepper to taste
- ✧ 2 ripe avocados
- ✧ Juice of 1 lemon
- ✧ 2 garlic cloves, chopped
- ✧ A pinch of salt and pepper

Directions:

- ✧ Preheat the oven to 425°F and line a baking sheet with parchment paper.
- ✧ Cut sweet potatoes into fry-shaped strips, toss with olive oil, rosemary, salt, and pepper, and spread them out on the sheet.
- ✧ Bake for 20-25 minutes, flipping occasionally, until crispy.
- ✧ For the dip, mash avocados with lemon juice, garlic, salt, and pepper.
- ✧ Serve the hot sweet potato fries with the avocado dip.

Nutritional Information per Serving - Calories: 400' Fat: 25 g Sodium: 450 mg Carbohydrates: 40 g Protein: 5 g Fiber: 10 g

Baked Zucchini Slices with Garlic Yogurt Dip

 10 Min  20 Min 4

These crispy baked zucchini slices are a healthy and flavorful snack, perfect for any time of the day. Paired with a creamy garlic yogurt dip, they offer a delicious alternative to traditional fried snacks.

Ingredients:

- ✧ 2 medium zucchinis
- ✧ 2 tablespoons olive oil
- ✧ A pinch of salt and pepper
- ✧ 2 teaspoons dried Italian herbs (optional)
- ✧ 1/2 cup Greek yogurt
- ✧ 2 garlic cloves, minced
- ✧ Juice of 1/2 lemon
- ✧ A pinch of salt and pepper
- ✧ Fresh parsley or dill for garnish (optional)

Directions:

- ✧ Preheat the oven to 425°F and line a baking sheet with parchment paper.
- ✧ Slice the zucchinis into thin rounds. In a bowl, toss the zucchini slices with olive oil, salt, pepper, and optional dried herbs until evenly coated.
- ✧ Arrange the zucchini slices in a single layer on the prepared baking sheet.
- ✧ Bake for 15-20 minutes, flipping halfway through, until the slices are golden brown and crispy.
- ✧ While the zucchini slices are baking, prepare the garlic yogurt dip.
- ✧ In a small bowl, combine the Greek yogurt with minced garlic, lemon juice, salt, and pepper.
- ✧ Stir well. Serve the hot baked zucchini slices with the garlic yogurt dip on the side, garnished with fresh parsley or dill if desired.

Nutritional Information per Serving - Calories: 150 Fat: 8 g Sodium: 250 mg Carbohydrates: 12 g Protein: 6 g Fiber: 3 g

Sautéed Edamame with Sea Salt and Lime Zest

 5 Min   10 Min   ✕✕ 4

Ingredients:

✧ 2 cups (about 7 oz) frozen edamame (young soybeans)
✧ 1 tablespoon olive oil
✧ Sea salt to taste
✧ Zest of 1/2 lime

This sautéed edamame is a quick and flavorful snack, perfect for a light bite or an appetizer. The combination of sea salt and fresh lime zest adds a zesty twist that enhances the natural flavor of the edamame.

Directions:

✧ Rinse the frozen edamame under cold running water in a colander and drain well.
✧ Heat a skillet over medium heat and add the olive oil. Once the oil is hot, add the drained edamame and sauté for about 8-10 minutes, stirring occasionally, until they are heated through and slightly browned.
✧ Remove the sautéed edamame from the skillet and place them on a paper towel to drain any excess oil.
✧ Transfer the edamame to a serving dish, sprinkle with sea salt, and evenly distribute the lime zest over the top.

Nutritional Information per Serving - Calories: 220' Fat: 10 g Sodium: 15 mg Carbohydrates: 15 g Protein: 15 g Fiber: 8 g

Tomato Basil Bruschetta on Whole Grain Bread

 10 Min   5 Min   ✕✕ 4

Ingredients:

✧ 8 slices whole grain bread
✧ 4 ripe tomatoes
✧ 2 garlic cloves
✧ A handful of fresh basil leaves
✧ 4 tablespoons extra virgin olive oil
✧ A pinch of salt and pepper

This fresh and flavorful tomato basil bruschetta is served on toasted whole grain bread, making it a healthy and delicious appetizer or snack. The combination of ripe tomatoes, fragrant basil, and a hint of garlic will delight your taste buds.

Directions:

✧ Preheat your oven's broiler.
✧ Wash the tomatoes, remove the cores, and dice them into small pieces.
✧ Wash and finely chop the basil leaves.
✧ Peel the garlic cloves and cut them in half.
✧ Rub the cut side of one garlic clove over each slice of whole grain bread.
✧ Place the garlic-rubbed bread slices on a baking sheet and broil them for about 2-3 minutes, or until they are lightly browned.
✧ Remove the toasted bread from the oven and place it on a serving platter.
✧ In a bowl, combine the diced tomatoes, chopped basil, olive oil, salt, and pepper, mixing well.
✧ Spoon the tomato-basil mixture evenly over the toasted bread slices.
✧ Garnish with additional fresh basil leaves if desired. Serve the tomato basil bruschetta immediately and enjoy!

Nutritional Information per Serving - Calories: 250 Fat: 10 g Sodium: 380 mg Carbohydrates: 35 g Protein: 8 g Fiber: 6 g

Cucumber Rolls with Cream Cheese and Smoked Salmon

 15 Min 0 Min ✗ 4

These refreshing cucumber rolls filled with herb cream cheese and smoked salmon are a light and elegant appetizer. Perfect for entertaining, they are quick to make and offer a delightful combination of flavors.

Ingredients:

✧ 1 large cucumber
✧ 3.5 oz herb cream cheese
✧ 3.5 oz smoked salmon
✧ Fresh herbs (e.g., dill, parsley) for garnish
✧ A few radish slices (optional)
✧ Salt and pepper to taste

Directions:

✧ Wash the cucumber and use a vegetable peeler to slice it lengthwise into thin strips.
✧ Spread the herb cream cheese evenly over the cucumber strips.
✧ Layer the smoked salmon on top of the cream cheese. Carefully roll up each cucumber strip and secure with a toothpick if needed.
✧ Arrange the cucumber rolls on a serving plate and garnish with fresh herbs.
✧ Optionally, add a few radish slices for decoration and season with salt and pepper.
✧ Serve immediately and enjoy these light and tasty bites!

Nutritional Information per Serving - Calories: 180'
Fat: 10 g Sodium: 800 mg Carbohydrates: 8 g Protein:
12 g Fiber: 2 g

Corn and Bell Pepper Fritters with Avocado Salsa

These crispy corn and bell pepper fritters are a delightful snack or appetizer, perfectly paired with a zesty avocado salsa. The fritters are easy to make and full of flavor, making them a great choice for any occasion.

 15 Min 10 Min ✗ 4

Directions:

✧ In a large bowl, mix cornmeal, whole wheat flour, baking powder, salt, and paprika.
✧ Stir in milk and egg until smooth, then fold in corn, bell pepper, and green onions.
✧ Heat olive oil in a skillet and cook tablespoon-sized fritters for 3-4 minutes per side until golden.
✧ For the salsa, mash avocado and mix with lime juice, cilantro, salt, and pepper.
✧ Serve fritters with avocado salsa.

Ingredients:

✧ 1/2 cup cornmeal
✧ 1/4 cup whole wheat flour
✧ 1/2 teaspoon baking powder
✧ 1/4 teaspoon salt
✧ 1/4 teaspoon paprika
✧ 1/4 cup milk or plant-based milk
✧ 1 large egg
✧ 1/4 cup corn kernels (canned or fresh)
✧ 1/4 cup chopped red bell pepper
✧ 1 tablespoon chopped green onions
✧ 1 tablespoon olive oil for frying
✧ 1 ripe avocado
✧ Juice of 1/2 lime
✧ 1 tablespoon chopped fresh cilantro
✧ Salt and pepper to taste

Nutritional Information per Serving - Calories: 400 Fat: 25 g Sodium: 450 mg Carbohydrates: 35 g Protein: 10 g Fiber:

Baked Eggplant Slices with Tahini Yogurt Sauce

 10 Min 20 Min ✗ 4

These baked eggplant slices are tender and flavorful, complemented perfectly by a creamy tahini yogurt sauce. This dish makes for a healthy and delicious appetizer or side, ideal for any occasion.

Ingredients:

✧ 1 small eggplant
✧ 1 tablespoon olive oil
✧ A pinch of salt and pepper
✧ 1 teaspoon dried Italian herbs (optional)
✧ 2 tablespoons Greek yogurt
✧ 1 tablespoon tahini (sesame paste)
✧ Juice of 1/2 lemon
✧ 1 garlic clove, minced
✧ A pinch of salt and pepper

Directions:

✧ Preheat the oven to 400°F and line a baking sheet with parchment paper.
✧ Slice the eggplant into 1/2-inch thick rounds and place on the sheet.
✧ Drizzle with olive oil, season with salt, pepper, and optional herbs.
✧ Bake for 15-20 minutes, flipping halfway through, until tender and browned.
✧ Meanwhile, mix Greek yogurt, tahini, lemon juice, garlic, salt, and pepper to make the sauce.
✧ Serve the roasted eggplant with the tahini yogurt sauce drizzled on top or as a dip.

Nutritional Information per Serving - Calories: 250' Fat: 8 g Sodium: 260 mg Carbohydrates: 20 g Protein: 7 g Fiber: 6 g

Ingredients:

✧ 3.5 oz cooked beets
✧ 1/2 can (about 3.5 oz) chickpeas, drained and rinsed
✧ 1 garlic clove, chopped
✧ Juice of 1/2 lemon
✧ 2 tablespoons tahini (sesame paste)
✧ 1 tablespoon olive oil
✧ A pinch of salt and pepper
✧ Optional: cumin or smoked paprika for seasoning
✧ 4 pita breads
✧ A handful of fresh arugula

Beet Hummus on Pita Bread with Arugula

 15 Min  0 Min ✗ 4

This vibrant beet hummus spread on warm pita bread is topped with fresh arugula for a flavorful and healthy snack or light meal. The beet hummus adds a sweet and earthy twist to the classic recipe, making it both visually appealing and delicious.

Directions:

✧ To make the beet hummus, combine all the ingredients in a blender or food processor and blend until smooth.
✧ Add a little water if needed to reach your desired consistency.
✧ Warm or toast the pita bread. Spread a generous amount of beet hummus over each pita bread, then top with fresh arugula.
✧ Fold or roll the pita bread, and serve immediately.
✧ Optionally, garnish with extra spices or fresh herbs for added flavor.

Nutritional Information per Serving - Calories: 180 Fat: 10 g Sodium: 120 mg Carbohydrates: 15 g Protein: 6 g Fiber: 5 g

Asparagus Bacon Wraps with Lemon Dill Dip

 15 Min 10 Min ✕ 4

These asparagus bacon wraps are a delightful appetizer or side dish, combining the savory flavor of crispy bacon with tender asparagus. Paired with a refreshing lemon dill dip, they make for an irresistible treat.

Ingredients:

- ✧ 24 spears green asparagus
- ✧ 12 slices thin-cut bacon
- ✧ 1 tablespoon olive oil
- ✧ Salt and pepper to taste
- ✧ 1/2 cup Greek yogurt
- ✧ 1 teaspoon fresh dill, chopped
- ✧ 1 teaspoon lemon juice
- ✧ A pinch of salt and pepper

Directions:

- ✧ Wash the asparagus, trim the ends, and peel if necessary.
- ✧ Halve the bacon slices to create 24 strips.
- ✧ Wrap each asparagus spear with a bacon strip. Heat a skillet over medium heat and add the olive oil.
- ✧ Place the asparagus bacon wraps in the skillet and cook for about 8-10 minutes, turning occasionally, until the bacon is crispy and the asparagus is tender.
- ✧ Meanwhile, prepare the lemon dill dip by mixing the Greek yogurt, chopped dill, lemon juice, salt, and pepper in a small bowl.
- ✧ Arrange the cooked asparagus bacon wraps on a serving plate and serve with the lemon dill dip on the side.
- ✧ Garnish with additional fresh herbs or lemon zest if desired.

Nutritional Information per Serving - Calories: 250' Fat: 8 g Sodium: 850 mg Carbohydrates: 45 g Protein: 15 g Fiber: 8 g

Poached Eggs with Spinach on Whole Grain Toast

 10 Min 5 Min ✕ 4

This simple yet elegant dish combines perfectly poached eggs with fresh spinach on top of hearty whole grain toast. It's a nutritious and delicious breakfast or brunch option that's easy to prepare.

Ingredients:

- ✧ 8 eggs
- ✧ 4 handfuls fresh spinach
- ✧ 4 slices whole grain bread
- ✧ 1 tablespoon vinegar (for poaching water)
- ✧ Salt and pepper to taste
- ✧ Optional: crushed red pepper flakes for garnish

Directions:

- ✧ Bring a pot of water to a boil and add a splash of vinegar.
- ✧ Reduce the heat so the water is just simmering.
- ✧ While the water heats, wash and drain the fresh spinach.
- ✧ Toast the whole grain bread slices and place them on serving plates.
- ✧ Crack each egg into a small bowl. Gently slide one egg at a time into the simmering water, using a spoon to carefully fold the egg white around the yolk.
- ✧ Poach for about 3-4 minutes, depending on your desired firmness.
- ✧ Remove the spinach with a slotted spoon and drain on a paper towel.
- ✧ Arrange the spinach on the toasted bread slices. Carefully remove the poached eggs from the water and place them on top of the spinach.
- ✧ Season with salt, pepper, and optional crushed red pepper flakes.
- ✧ Serve immediately and enjoy!

Nutritional Information per Serving - Calories: 200 Fat: 10 g Sodium: 420 mg Carbohydrates: 15 g Protein: 15 g Fiber: 5 g

Chapter 5

Soups and Stews for Anti-Inflammation

In Chapter 5, we dive into the comforting and nourishing world of soups and stews, specially crafted to help reduce inflammation and promote overall health. These recipes combine the warmth and coziness of classic comfort food with the power of anti-inflammatory ingredients, creating meals that soothe both body and soul. Each recipe is designed to be not only delicious but also packed with ingredients known for their anti-inflammatory properties, such as ginger, turmeric, leafy greens, and protein-rich legumes.

From classics like creamy carrot-ginger soup to robust lentil and chickpea stews, these recipes are sure to become staples in your kitchen, providing you with both comfort and nutrition as you support your healthy lifestyle. Embrace the therapeutic warmth of these soups and stews, and experience the restorative benefits they bring to your table, helping you feel your best every day.

Turmeric Coconut Lentil Soup

 10 Min   20 Min    4

This creamy turmeric coconut lentil soup is packed with anti-inflammatory ingredients and full of warming flavors. It's a perfect quick meal that's both nourishing and satisfying.

Ingredients:

✧ 1/2 cup red lentils
✧ 1 cup coconut milk
✧ 1 cup vegetable broth
✧ 1 teaspoon turmeric
✧ 1/2 teaspoon ground ginger
✧ 1 garlic clove, minced
✧ 1 tablespoon olive oil
✧ Salt and pepper to taste
✧ Fresh cilantro leaves for garnish (optional)

Directions:

✧ Rinse the red lentils thoroughly under cold running water and drain well.
✧ In a pot, heat the olive oil over medium heat and sauté the minced garlic until fragrant.
✧ Add the drained lentils and stir for a minute with the garlic. Stir in the turmeric and ground ginger, mixing well to coat the lentils.
✧ Pour in the coconut milk and vegetable broth, stirring to combine, and bring the mixture to a boil.
✧ Reduce the heat and simmer the soup for 15-20 minutes, or until the lentils are tender.
✧ Season with salt and pepper to taste. Serve the soup in bowls, garnished with fresh cilantro leaves if desired.

Nutritional Information per Serving - Calories: 350 Fat: 20 g Sodium: 650 mg Carbohydrates: 30 g Protein: 12 g Fiber: 10 g

Ginger Carrot Stew with Chickpeas

 15 Min   25 Min   ✗ 4

Ingredients:

- ✧ 1 large carrot, peeled and sliced
- ✧ 1/2 onion, chopped
- ✧ 1 garlic clove, minced
- ✧ 1 teaspoon freshly grated ginger
- ✧ 1 tablespoon olive oil
- ✧ 1 cup vegetable broth
- ✧ 1/2 cup cooked chickpeas (canned or homemade)
- ✧ Salt and pepper to taste
- ✧ Fresh parsley for garnish (optional)

This hearty ginger carrot stew is both comforting and nourishing, featuring the warm flavors of ginger and the earthiness of carrots. Paired with protein-rich chickpeas, it's a perfect meal for cooler days.

Directions:

- ✧ In a pot, heat the olive oil over medium heat and sauté the chopped onion until translucent.
- ✧ Add the minced garlic and grated ginger, cooking for another 1-2 minutes until fragrant.
- ✧ Stir in the carrot slices and cook for about 5 minutes, allowing them to brown slightly.
- ✧ Pour in the vegetable broth and bring the mixture to a boil. Reduce the heat and let the stew simmer for 15-20 minutes, until the carrots are tender.
- ✧ Add the cooked chickpeas and heat through. Season with salt and pepper to taste.
- ✧ Serve the stew in bowls, garnished with fresh parsley if desired.

Nutritional Information per Serving – Calories: 300' Fat: 10 g Sodium: 400 mg Carbohydrates: 40 g Protein: 10 g Fiber: 8 g

Green Pea and Mint Soup with Avocado

 10 Min   15 Min   ✗ 4

Ingredients:

- ✧ 1 1/2 cups frozen green peas
- ✧ 1/2 avocado, peeled and pitted
- ✧ 1 small onion, chopped
- ✧ 1 garlic clove, minced
- ✧ 1 handful fresh mint leaves
- ✧ 1 1/4 cups vegetable broth
- ✧ Juice of 1/2 lemon
- ✧ Salt and pepper to taste
- ✧ A drizzle of olive oil
- ✧ Fresh mint leaves for garnish (optional)

This refreshing green pea and mint soup is creamy and light, with the added richness of avocado. It's perfect for a quick lunch or as a starter to a larger meal.

Directions:

- ✧ In a pot, heat the olive oil over medium heat and sauté the chopped onion and minced garlic until translucent.
- ✧ Add the frozen green peas and sauté for 2-3 minutes until they thaw.
- ✧ Pour in the vegetable broth and bring to a boil. Reduce the heat and simmer for 10 minutes, until the peas are tender.
- ✧ While the soup simmers, cut the avocado into small chunks. Add the fresh mint leaves to the soup and blend with an immersion blender or in a regular blender until smooth.
- ✧ Stir in the avocado pieces and lemon juice. Season with salt and pepper to taste.
- ✧ Serve the soup in bowls, garnished with fresh mint leaves if desired.

Nutritional Information per Serving – Calories: 600 Fat: 15 g Sodium: 670 mg Carbohydrates: 30 g Protein: 8 g Fiber: 10 g

Tomato Basil Soup with Quinoa

 10 Min 20 Min  4

This hearty tomato basil soup is elevated with the addition of quinoa, making it both satisfying and nutritious. It's perfect for a cozy lunch or light dinner and can be enriched with a splash of cream or coconut milk for extra creaminess.

Ingredients:

✧ 7 oz ripe tomatoes, roughly chopped
✧ 1 small onion, chopped
✧ 1 garlic clove, minced
✧ 1/4 cup quinoa
✧ 1 1/4 cups vegetable broth
✧ A few fresh basil leaves, chopped
✧ Salt and pepper to taste
✧ A drizzle of olive oil
✧ Optional: A splash of cream or coconut milk for added richness

Directions:

✧ In a pot, heat the olive oil over medium heat and sauté the chopped onion and minced garlic until softened.
✧ Add the chopped tomatoes and cook for about 5 minutes, until they start to break down.
✧ Stir in the quinoa and vegetable broth, bringing the mixture to a boil.
✧ Reduce the heat and simmer for 15 minutes, or until the quinoa is tender.
✧ Remove the pot from the heat and use an immersion blender or regular blender to purée the soup to a smooth consistency.
✧ Stir in the chopped basil and season with salt and pepper.
✧ For a richer flavor, add a splash of cream or coconut milk.
✧ Serve the soup in bowls, garnished with additional fresh basil if desired.

Nutritional Information per Serving - Calories: 250 Fat: 5 g Sodium: 670 mg Carbohydrates: 40 g Protein: 7 g Fiber: 6 g

Sweet Potato Ginger Curry Soup

 10 Min 25 Min  4

This vibrant sweet potato ginger curry soup is a comforting blend of flavors, with the warming spices of curry and the creaminess of coconut milk. It's perfect for a cozy meal any time of the year.

Ingredients:

✧ 1 medium sweet potato, peeled and diced
✧ 1 small onion, chopped
✧ 1 garlic clove, minced
✧ 1 teaspoon fresh ginger, grated
✧ 1 teaspoon curry powder
✧ 1 1/4 cups vegetable broth
✧ 1/4 cup coconut milk
✧ A drizzle of olive oil
✧ Salt and pepper to taste
✧ Fresh cilantro for garnish (optional)

Nutritional Information per Serving - Calories: 250 Fat: 8 g Sodium: 650 mg Carbohydrates: 40 g Protein: 4 g Fiber: 6 g

Directions:

✧ In a pot, heat the olive oil over medium heat and sauté the chopped onion until translucent.
✧ Add the minced garlic and grated ginger, cooking for an additional 1-2 minutes until fragrant.
✧ Stir in the curry powder and cook for another minute to release the spices' aroma.
✧ Add the diced sweet potato and toss to coat with the spices. Pour in the vegetable broth and bring the mixture to a boil.
✧ Reduce the heat and simmer for about 15-20 minutes, until the sweet potatoes are tender.
✧ Remove the pot from the heat and purée the soup using an immersion blender or in a regular blender until smooth.
✧ Stir in the coconut milk until well combined. Season with salt and pepper to taste.
✧ Serve the soup in bowls, garnished with fresh cilantro if desired.

Spinach Coconut Stew with Shrimp

 10 Min   20 Min 🍴 4

This rich and flavorful spinach coconut stew with shrimp combines the creamy sweetness of coconut milk with the freshness of spinach and the delicate flavor of shrimp. It's a perfect dish for a cozy dinner.

Ingredients:

- ✧ 7 oz shrimp, peeled and deveined
- ✧ 3.5 oz fresh spinach
- ✧ 1/2 cup coconut milk
- ✧ 1 small onion, chopped
- ✧ 1 garlic clove, minced
- ✧ 1 teaspoon fresh ginger, grated
- ✧ 1 teaspoon curry powder
- ✧ 3/4 cup vegetable broth
- ✧ A drizzle of olive oil
- ✧ Salt and pepper to taste
- ✧ Fresh cilantro for garnish (optional)

Directions:

- ✧ In a pot, heat the olive oil over medium heat and sauté the chopped onion until translucent.
- ✧ Add the minced garlic and grated ginger, cooking for an additional 1-2 minutes until fragrant.
- ✧ Stir in the curry powder and cook for another minute to release the spices' aroma.
- ✧ Add the shrimp and cook for about 3-4 minutes until they turn pink and are fully cooked through. Remove the shrimp from the pot and set aside.
- ✧ Add the fresh spinach to the pot and sauté until wilted. Pour in the coconut milk and vegetable broth, bringing the mixture to a boil.
- ✧ Reduce the heat and simmer the stew for about 10 minutes to allow the flavors to meld. Return the shrimp to the pot and stir to combine.
- ✧ Season with salt and pepper to taste. Serve the stew in bowls, garnished with fresh cilantro if desired.

Nutritional Information per Serving - Calories: 300' Fat: 20 g Sodium: 600 mg Carbohydrates: 10 g Protein: 20 g Fiber: 8 g

Broccoli Almond Soup with Roasted Chickpeas

 10 Min   20 Min 🍴 4

This creamy broccoli almond soup, topped with crispy roasted chickpeas, is a delightful blend of textures and flavors. It's both nourishing and satisfying—perfect for a cozy meal.

Ingredients:

- ✧ 2 cups broccoli florets
- ✧ 1 small onion, chopped
- ✧ 1 garlic clove, minced
- ✧ 1 3/4 cups vegetable broth
- ✧ 1/4 cup almonds, chopped
- ✧ 1/4 cup cooked chickpeas
- ✧ 1 tablespoon olive oil
- ✧ Salt and pepper to taste
- ✧ Fresh chives for garnish (optional)

Directions:

- ✧ In a pot, heat the olive oil over medium heat and sauté the chopped onion until translucent.
- ✧ Add the minced garlic and cook for another 1-2 minutes until fragrant.
- ✧ Stir in the broccoli florets and cook for a few minutes before adding the vegetable broth.
- ✧ Bring the mixture to a boil, then reduce the heat and simmer for about 15 minutes, or until the broccoli is tender.
- ✧ While the soup is simmering, spread the chickpeas on a baking sheet and roast them at 400°F for about 15 minutes until crispy.
- ✧ Toast the chopped almonds in a dry skillet until golden brown. Remove the soup from heat and purée it with an immersion blender or in a regular blender until smooth.
- ✧ Season the soup with salt and pepper to taste.
- ✧ Serve the soup in bowls, topped with roasted chickpeas, toasted almonds, and a sprinkle of fresh chives if desired.

Nutritional Information per Serving - Calories: 350 Fat: 20 g Sodium: 700 mg Carbohydrates: 30 g Protein: 12 g Fiber: 10 g

Pumpkin Coconut Curry Stew

 15 Min 25 Min ✗ 4

This warm and comforting pumpkin coconut curry stew is rich in flavor and perfect for a cozy meal. The blend of spices with creamy coconut milk and tender pumpkin makes this dish irresistible.

Ingredients:

✧ 2 cups pumpkin, cubed
✧ 1 small onion, chopped
✧ 1 garlic clove, minced
✧ 3/4 cup coconut milk
✧ 3/4 cup vegetable broth
✧ 1 teaspoon curry powder
✧ 1 teaspoon ground ginger
✧ 1 teaspoon turmeric
✧ Salt and pepper to taste
✧ 1 tablespoon coconut oil
✧ Fresh cilantro for garnish (optional)

Directions:

✧ In a large pot, heat the coconut oil over medium heat and sauté the chopped onion until translucent.
✧ Add the minced garlic and cook for another 1-2 minutes until fragrant.
✧ Stir in the pumpkin cubes and cook for a few minutes before adding the vegetable broth and coconut milk.
✧ Stir in the curry powder, ground ginger, and turmeric, making sure everything is well mixed.
✧ Reduce the heat and let the stew simmer for about 20 minutes, or until the pumpkin is tender.
✧ Season with salt and pepper to taste.
✧ Serve the stew in bowls, garnished with fresh cilantro if desired. Enjoy it hot!

Nutritional Information per Serving - Calories: 350' Fat: 25 g Sodium: 550 mg Carbohydrates: 30 g Protein: 8 g Fiber: 8 g

Beetroot Coconut Soup with Ginger

 10 Min 25 Min ✗ 4

This vibrant beetroot coconut soup is infused with fresh ginger for a warming and nourishing dish. The natural sweetness of the beets pairs beautifully with the creaminess of the coconut milk, creating a unique and delightful flavor.

Ingredients:

✧ 2 cups beetroot, peeled and diced
✧ 1 small onion, chopped
✧ 1 garlic clove, minced
✧ 3/4 cup coconut milk
✧ 3/4 cup vegetable broth
✧ 1 teaspoon fresh ginger, grated
✧ 1 tablespoon coconut oil
✧ Salt and pepper to taste
✧ Fresh cilantro for garnish (optional)

Directions:

✧ In a large pot, heat the coconut oil over medium heat. Add the chopped onion and sauté until translucent.
✧ Stir in the minced garlic and grated ginger, cooking for an additional 1-2 minutes until fragrant.
✧ Add the diced beetroot and cook briefly before pouring in the vegetable broth and coconut milk.
✧ Bring the mixture to a boil, then reduce the heat and simmer for about 20 minutes, or until the beetroot is tender.
✧ Remove from heat and use an immersion blender to puree the soup until smooth and creamy.
✧ Adjust the consistency with additional water or broth if needed. Season with salt and pepper to taste.
✧ Serve the soup in bowls, garnished with fresh cilantro if desired. Enjoy it hot!

Nutritional Information per Serving - Calories: 250 Fat: 20 g Sodium: 670 mg Carbohydrates: 15 g Protein: 4 g Fiber: 4 g

Celery-Apple Soup with Walnuts

 15 Min 25 Min ✗ 4

Ingredients:

✧ 1/2 celery root, peeled and diced
✧ 1 tart apple, peeled, cored, and diced
✧ 1 small onion, chopped
✧ 1 garlic clove, minced
✧ 3/4 cup vegetable broth
✧ 1/2 cup coconut milk
✧ 1 tablespoon olive oil
✧ Salt and pepper to taste
✧ A handful of walnut halves, roughly chopped, for garnish
✧ Fresh chives or parsley, finely chopped, for garnish

This creamy celery-apple soup is perfectly balanced with the sweetness of apple and the earthy flavor of celery, topped with crunchy walnuts for added texture. It's a comforting dish that's both light and nourishing.

Directions:

✧ In a large pot, heat the olive oil over medium heat and sauté the chopped onion until it becomes translucent.
✧ Add the minced garlic and cook for another 1-2 minutes until fragrant.
✧ Stir in the diced celery root and apple, cooking until they start to brown slightly.
✧ Pour in the vegetable broth, bring the mixture to a boil, then reduce the heat and let it simmer for about 20 minutes, or until the vegetables are tender.
✧ Remove from heat and blend the soup until smooth using an immersion blender.
✧ Stir in the coconut milk and season with salt and pepper to taste.
✧ Serve the soup hot, garnished with chopped walnuts and fresh chives or parsley.

Nutritional Information per Serving - Calories: 300' Fat: 20 g Sodium: 700 mg Carbohydrates: 25 g Protein: 4 g Fiber: 6 g

Zucchini and Bell Pepper Stew with Quinoa

 10 Min 25 Min ✗ 4

Ingredients:

✧ 1 small zucchini, sliced
✧ 1 red bell pepper, cored and sliced into strips
✧ 1 small onion, chopped
✧ 1 garlic clove, minced
✧ 1/4 cup quinoa, rinsed
✧ 3/4 cup vegetable broth
✧ 1 tablespoon olive oil
✧ 1 teaspoon ground cumin
✧ Salt and pepper to taste
✧ Fresh parsley or cilantro, chopped, for garnish

This hearty, veggie-packed zucchini and bell pepper stew is enhanced with the nutty flavor of quinoa, making it a satisfying and wholesome meal perfect for any time of the year. Garnish with fresh herbs for an added burst of flavor.

Directions:

✧ In a large pot, heat olive oil over medium heat and sauté the chopped onion until softened.
✧ Add minced garlic and cook for 1-2 minutes. Stir in zucchini slices and bell pepper strips, cooking until slightly browned.
✧ Add rinsed quinoa and ground cumin, then pour in vegetable broth.
✧ Bring to a boil, reduce heat, and simmer for 15-20 minutes until vegetables are tender and quinoa is cooked.
✧ Season with salt and pepper and serve garnished with fresh parsley or cilantro.

Nutritional Information per Serving - Calories: 300 Fat: 8 g Sodium: 680 mg Carbohydrates: 45 g Protein: 9 g Fiber: 8 g

Spinach and Chickpea Stew with Tomatoes

 10 Min   20 Min   ✗ 4

This hearty and nutritious stew combines fresh spinach and protein-rich chickpeas in a savory tomato broth. It's simple to make and can be garnished with fresh lemon juice and herbs for a bright, flavorful finish.

Ingredients:

- ✧ 1 tablespoon olive oil
- ✧ 1 small onion, chopped
- ✧ 1 garlic clove, minced
- ✧ 1 small can (approx. 15 oz) chickpeas, drained and rinsed
- ✧ 7 oz fresh spinach, roughly chopped
- ✧ 7 oz canned diced tomatoes (or fresh)
- ✧ 3/4 cup vegetable broth
- ✧ 1 teaspoon ground cumin
- ✧ Salt and pepper to taste
- ✧ Fresh lemon juice for garnish
- ✧ Fresh cilantro or parsley, chopped, for garnish

Directions:

- ✧ Heat olive oil in a large pot over medium heat and sauté the chopped onion until translucent.
- ✧ Add the minced garlic and cook for 1-2 minutes until fragrant.
- ✧ Stir in the chickpeas, diced tomatoes, and ground cumin, mixing everything well.
- ✧ Pour in the vegetable broth and bring to a boil. Reduce the heat and let it simmer for about 15 minutes until the tomatoes break down and the chickpeas soften.
- ✧ Add the chopped spinach and cook for another 5 minutes, allowing the spinach to wilt. Season with salt and pepper to taste.
- ✧ Serve the stew in bowls, garnished with a squeeze of fresh lemon juice and a sprinkle of chopped cilantro or parsley.

Nutritional Information per Serving - Calories: 300' Fat: 10 g Sodium: 720 mg Carbohydrates: 40 g Protein: 12 g Fiber: 12 g

Barley Soup with Mushrooms and Thyme

 10 Min   30 Min   ✗ 4

This hearty barley soup with mushrooms and thyme is a comforting, flavorful dish that is perfect for cooler days. The combination of earthy mushrooms and fresh herbs makes it a wholesome and delicious meal.

Ingredients:

- ✧ 1/4 cup pearl barley
- ✧ 3/4 cup vegetable broth
- ✧ 1 tbsp olive oil
- ✧ 1 small onion, chopped
- ✧ 1 garlic clove, minced
- ✧ 1 cup mixed mushrooms (e.g., button mushrooms, shiitake), sliced
- ✧ 1 tbsp fresh thyme, chopped
- ✧ Salt and pepper to taste
- ✧ Fresh parsley, chopped, for garnish

Directions:

- ✧ Rinse the pearl barley thoroughly and drain. In a pot, bring the vegetable broth to a boil, then add the barley.
- ✧ Simmer over medium heat for about 20 minutes, until the barley is nearly tender.
- ✧ Meanwhile, heat olive oil in a pan and sauté the chopped onion until translucent.
- ✧ Add the minced garlic and cook for another 1-2 minutes. Add the mushrooms and sauté until soft and lightly browned.
- ✧ Transfer the sautéed mushrooms to the pot with the barley. Stir in the fresh thyme and mix well.
- ✧ Season the soup with salt and pepper, then simmer for an additional 5-10 minutes, until the barley is fully cooked and the flavors have melded together.
- ✧ Serve the soup hot, garnished with fresh chopped parsley.

Nutritional Information per Serving- Calories: 250 Fat: 7 g Sodium: 600 mg Carbohydrates: 40 g Protein: 8 g Fiber: 8 g

Chapter 6

Main Dishes Free from Inflammatory Triggers

In this chapter, we dive into the heart of every meal—the main course. These recipes are designed to satisfy your hunger and provide the essential nutrients your body needs, all while keeping inflammation at bay. Each dish is crafted to deliver a satisfying and nourishing meal, packed with ingredients known for their powerful anti-inflammatory properties. Say goodbye to common triggers like refined sugars, processed grains, and unhealthy fats that can lead to chronic inflammation, and instead embrace meals that nourish your body from the inside out. Our main course recipes put the spotlight on whole foods that are rich in antioxidants, healthy fats, and lean proteins. You'll find a variety of dishes that incorporate fresh vegetables, omega-3-rich fish, plant-based proteins, and heart-healthy oils like olive and avocado. These meals are not only delicious but also carefully balanced to support your overall well-being and provide long-lasting energy. Whether you're in the mood for a light, vibrant salad or a hearty, protein-packed dinner, this chapter has you covered.

Salmon Fillet with Broccoli and Quinoa

 10 Min   20 Min    4

This healthy and balanced meal combines tender salmon, protein-packed quinoa, and nutrient-rich broccoli for a delicious anti-inflammatory dinner. It's perfect for a quick weeknight meal or a nutritious lunch.

Ingredients:

✧ 1 salmon fillet (approx. 5 oz)
✧ 1/2 cup quinoa
✧ 1 cup broccoli florets
✧ 1 garlic clove, minced
✧ 1 tbsp olive oil
✧ Salt and pepper to taste
✧ Fresh lemon juice (optional)
✧ Fresh herbs for garnish (e.g., parsley or dill)

Directions:

✧ Rinse the quinoa thoroughly under cold water.
✧ In a saucepan, combine quinoa with 1 cup of water and bring to a boil. Reduce heat and simmer for about 15 minutes until quinoa is tender and water is absorbed.
✧ Meanwhile, blanch the broccoli florets in salted boiling water until tender yet crisp, then drain and set aside.
✧ Season the salmon fillet with salt and pepper. Heat olive oil in a skillet over medium heat, sauté garlic until fragrant, then cook the salmon fillet for 3-4 minutes per side, until golden and cooked through.
✧ Serve the salmon over the cooked quinoa, surrounded by the broccoli.
✧ Drizzle with fresh lemon juice and garnish with herbs if desired. Enjoy immediately!

Nutritional Information per Serving - Calories: 450 Fat: 20 g Sodium: 800 mg Carbohydrates: 30 g Protein: 35 g Fiber: 8 g

Vegetable Coconut Curry

 10 Min 20 Min 4

Ingredients:

- ✧ 4 cups mixed vegetables of choice (e.g., carrots, bell peppers, zucchini, peas)
- ✧ 2 tbsp coconut oil
- ✧ 1 medium onion, chopped
- ✧ 2 garlic cloves, minced
- ✧ 1 tbsp fresh ginger, grated
- ✧ 1 tbsp curry powder
- ✧ 1 can (14 oz) unsweetened coconut milk
- ✧ Salt and pepper to taste
- ✧ Fresh cilantro for garnish (optional)
- ✧ Cooked rice or quinoa for serving

This creamy and flavorful vegetable coconut curry is packed with a variety of vegetables and fragrant spices. Serve it with rice or quinoa for a wholesome and satisfying meal.

Directions:

- ✧ Prepare the mixed vegetables by chopping them into bite-sized pieces. In a large pan, heat the coconut oil over medium heat.
- ✧ Add the chopped onion and sauté until softened, about 3-4 minutes.
- ✧ Stir in the minced garlic and grated ginger, cooking for an additional 1-2 minutes until fragrant.
- ✧ Add the vegetables to the pan and cook for 5 minutes, stirring occasionally, until they start to soften and brown slightly.
- ✧ Sprinkle the curry powder over the vegetables and stir well to coat evenly.
- ✧ Pour in the coconut milk, stirring to combine. Simmer the curry on low heat for 10-15 minutes until the vegetables are tender and the sauce has thickened.
- ✧ Season with salt and pepper to taste.
- ✧ Garnish with fresh cilantro and serve with cooked rice or quinoa.

Nutritional Information per Serving - Calories: 300' Fat: 25 g Sodium: 80 mg Carbohydrates: 15 g Protein: 5 g Fiber: 5 g

Baked Chicken Breast with Sweet Potato Mash

 15 Min 30 Min 4

Ingredients:

- ✧ 4 boneless, skinless chicken breasts (about 6 oz each)
- ✧ 2 large, sweet potatoes, peeled and cubed
- ✧ 2 tbsp olive oil
- ✧ Salt and pepper to taste
- ✧ 2 tsp paprika
- ✧ Fresh parsley or cilantro for garnish (optional)

This hearty and nutritious dish features tender baked chicken breast paired with creamy sweet potato mash. Garnish with fresh herbs for an extra burst of flavor.

Directions:

- ✧ Preheat the oven to 400°F. Boil the sweet potato cubes in a large pot of salted water for about 15 minutes, until soft.
- ✧ Drain the potatoes and mash them in a bowl with salt and pepper to taste.
- ✧ Meanwhile, season the chicken breasts with salt, pepper, and paprika.
- ✧ Heat 1 tablespoon of olive oil in a large skillet over medium heat. Sear the chicken breasts for 5-7 minutes on each side until golden brown.
- ✧ Transfer the chicken to a baking sheet and bake in the preheated oven for 10-15 minutes, or until fully cooked (internal temperature of 165°F).
- ✧ Serve the baked chicken breasts on top of the sweet potato mash, garnished with fresh parsley or cilantro.

Nutritional Information per Serving - Calories: 400 Fat: 30 g Sodium: 300 mg Carbohydrates: 30 g Protein: 15 g

Baked Sea Bass with Tomatoes and Olives

 10 Min   0 Min   4

This baked sea bass dish is light, fresh, and bursting with Mediterranean flavors from the tomatoes, olives, and garlic. Serve with a side of roasted vegetables or a simple salad for a well-balanced meal.

Ingredients:

✧ 4 sea bass fillets
✧ 1 cup cherry tomatoes, halved
✧ 24 pitted olives, sliced
✧ 4 garlic cloves, minced
✧ 4 tbsp olive oil
✧ 4 tsp lemon juice
✧ Salt and pepper to taste
✧ Fresh parsley or basil for garnish

Directions:

✧ Preheat the oven to 400°F and line a baking dish with parchment paper.
✧ Rinse and pat dry the sea bass fillets, then season them with salt, pepper, and lemon juice.
✧ In a bowl, combine the halved cherry tomatoes, sliced olives, and minced garlic.
✧ Drizzle with olive oil and lightly season with salt and pepper. Place the seasoned sea bass fillets on the prepared baking dish and arrange the tomato-olive mixture around them.
✧ Bake in the preheated oven for 15-20 minutes, or until the fish is cooked through and the tomatoes are slightly caramelized.
✧ Serve hot, garnished with fresh parsley or basil.

Nutritional Information per Serving - Calories: 300' Fat: 15 g Sodium: 620 mg Carbohydrates: 10 g

Spinach Ricotta Cannelloni with Whole Wheat Pasta

 20 Min   25 Min   4

These wholesome spinach and ricotta cannelloni, made with whole wheat pasta, offer a healthy and comforting meal. Topped with a rich tomato sauce and melted mozzarella, it's a perfect dish for a cozy dinner.

Ingredients:

✧ 16 whole wheat cannelloni tubes
✧ 6 cups fresh spinach, washed and roughly chopped
✧ 1 3/4 cups ricotta cheese
✧ 4 garlic cloves, minced
✧ 4 tbsp olive oil
✧ 3 1/2 cups crushed tomatoes
✧ 2 cups shredded mozzarella cheese
✧ Salt and pepper to taste
✧ Fresh basil leaves for garnish

Directions:

✧ Preheat the oven to 350°F.
✧ Cook the cannelloni tubes according to the package instructions until al dente. Drain and set aside.
✧ In a pan, heat the olive oil and sauté the minced garlic until fragrant. Add the spinach and cook until wilted, stirring occasionally. Remove from heat and let cool.
✧ In a bowl, mix the ricotta with the cooled spinach mixture, seasoning with salt and pepper.
✧ Fill the cannelloni tubes with the spinach-ricotta mixture and place them in a greased baking dish.
✧ Pour the crushed tomatoes over the cannelloni and top with shredded mozzarella.
✧ Bake in the preheated oven for 20-25 minutes, or until the cheese is golden and the sauce is bubbling.
✧ Serve hot, garnished with fresh basil leaves.

Nutritional Information per Serving - Calories: 400 Fat: 15 g Sodium: 700 mg Carbohydrates: 45 g Protein: 20 g Fiber: 7 g

Eggplant Parmesan with Tomato Sauce

 15 Min   30 Min  4

This comforting Eggplant Parmesan is baked to golden perfection and topped with a flavorful homemade tomato sauce. It's a deliciously rich and cheesy dish that's perfect for any weeknight dinner or family gathering.

Directions:

- ✧ Slice the eggplant into thin rounds and sprinkle with salt, letting it rest for 10 minutes to draw out bitterness.
- ✧ Preheat the oven to 400°F and lightly grease a baking sheet.
- ✧ Beat the eggs in one bowl, and in another, combine the breadcrumbs and grated Parmesan.
- ✧ Pat the eggplant slices dry with paper towels, then dip each slice into the beaten eggs followed by the breadcrumb mixture. Place the coated slices on the baking sheet and bake for 20-25 minutes until golden and crispy.
- ✧ Meanwhile, heat the olive oil in a pan and sauté the minced garlic until fragrant.
- ✧ Add the crushed tomatoes, basil, oregano, salt, and pepper, and simmer for 5-7 minutes until slightly thickened.
- ✧ Serve the baked eggplant slices topped with the tomato sauce and garnish with fresh basil.

Ingredients:

- ✧ 1 medium eggplant
- ✧ Salt
- ✧ 2 eggs
- ✧ 1/2 cup breadcrumbs
- ✧ 1/2 cup grated Parmesan cheese
- ✧ 1 1/4 cups crushed tomatoes
- ✧ 1 garlic clove, minced
- ✧ 1 tbsp olive oil
- ✧ 1 tsp dried basil
- ✧ 1 tsp dried oregano
- ✧ Salt and pepper to taste
- ✧ Fresh basil for garnish

Nutritional Information per Serving - Calories: 400' Fat: 15 g Sodium: 1200 mg Carbohydrates: 40 g Protein: 20 g Fiber: 10 g

Lemon-Herb Chicken with Roasted Asparagus

 10 Min  20 Min   4

This vibrant lemon-herb chicken pairs perfectly with tender roasted asparagus for a fresh, flavorful meal. Simple yet elegant, this dish can be served with a side of quinoa or rice for a complete dinner.

Directions:

- ✧ Preheat the oven to 400°F.
- ✧ Lightly pound the chicken breasts to even thickness and season with salt and pepper.
- ✧ In a bowl, mix the chopped parsley, minced garlic, lemon zest, lemon juice, and 2 tbsp olive oil.
- ✧ Coat the chicken in the lemon-herb mixture and allow it to marinate for a few minutes.
- ✧ Place the chicken on a parchment-lined baking sheet and bake for 20 minutes, or until cooked through.
- ✧ Meanwhile, spread the asparagus on another lined baking sheet, drizzle with the remaining olive oil, sprinkle with smoked paprika, salt, and pepper.
- ✧ Roast the asparagus for 10-12 minutes until tender and slightly browned.
- ✧ Serve the lemon-herb chicken with the roasted asparagus, garnished with lemon slices.

Ingredients:

- ✧ 4 boneless, skinless chicken breasts
- ✧ 1 bunch fresh parsley, chopped
- ✧ 4 garlic cloves, minced
- ✧ Zest and juice of 1 lemon
- ✧ 4 tbsp olive oil
- ✧ Salt and pepper to taste
- ✧ 21 oz green asparagus, tough ends trimmed
- ✧ 4 tsp smoked paprika
- ✧ Lemon slices for serving

Nutritional Information per Serving - Calories: 350 Fat: 20 g Sodium: 300 mg Carbohydrates: 10 g Protein: 30 g Fiber: 5 g

Lentil Dal with Sautéed Vegetables

 10 Min    0 Min   ✕ 4

This flavorful lentil dal combines the warm spices of cumin, turmeric, and garam masala with tender vegetables for a nutritious and comforting meal. Serve it with basmati or brown rice and garnish with fresh cilantro for a complete dish.

Ingredients:

- ✧ 1 cup red lentils
- ✧ 1 small onion, chopped
- ✧ 1 garlic clove, minced
- ✧ 1 tsp fresh ginger, grated
- ✧ 1 tsp cumin
- ✧ 1 tsp turmeric
- ✧ 1/2 tsp ground coriander
- ✧ 1/2 tsp garam masala
- ✧ 1 3/4 cups vegetable broth
- ✧ Salt and pepper, to taste
- ✧ 1 tbsp olive oil
- ✧ 1 cup mixed vegetables (e.g., bell pepper, zucchini, carrots), chopped
- ✧ Fresh cilantro, for garnish
- ✧ Cooked basmati or brown rice, for serving

Directions:

- ✧ Rinse red lentils and set aside.
- ✧ In a pot, heat olive oil over medium heat, sauté chopped onion for 3-4 minutes, then add minced garlic and grated ginger for 1-2 minutes.
- ✧ Stir in cumin, turmeric, ground coriander, and garam masala, toasting briefly.
- ✧ Add lentils and vegetable broth, bring to a boil, then simmer for 20-25 minutes until creamy.
- ✧ In a separate pan, sauté mixed vegetables until tender and browned.
- ✧ Stir vegetables into the lentil dal, season with salt and pepper, and serve over basmati or brown rice, garnished with fresh cilantro.

Nutritional Information per Serving - Calories: 300 Fat: 8 g Sodium: 1200 mg Carbohydrates: 40 g Protein: 15 g Fiber: 12 g

Beet and Goat Cheese Salad with Walnuts

 10 Min   45 Min   ✕ 4

This vibrant salad pairs the earthy sweetness of roasted beets with creamy goat cheese and crunchy walnuts. A light balsamic dressing ties it all together, making it a perfect appetizer or light meal.

Ingredients:

- ✧ 1 medium beet
- ✧ 2 oz goat cheese, sliced
- ✧ 1/4 cup walnuts, roughly chopped
- ✧ 4 cups mixed greens
- ✧ 1 tbsp olive oil
- ✧ 1 tbsp balsamic vinegar
- ✧ Salt and pepper, to taste
- ✧ Fresh parsley or chives, for garnish

Directions:

- ✧ Preheat the oven to 400°F.
- ✧ Wash and dry the beet, then pierce it several times with a knife or fork.
- ✧ Wrap the beet in aluminum foil and roast in the oven for about 45 minutes until tender.
- ✧ Allow the beet to cool, then peel and slice it.
- ✧ While the beet is roasting, prepare the salad by washing and drying the mixed greens and placing them in a large bowl. Scatter the goat cheese slices and chopped walnuts over the greens.
- ✧ In a small bowl, whisk together olive oil, balsamic vinegar, salt, and pepper.
- ✧ Once the beet is ready, place the slices on top of the salad. Drizzle the dressing over the salad and toss gently to coat everything evenly.
- ✧ Garnish with fresh parsley or chives and serve immediately.

Nutritional Information per Serving - Calories: 350 Fat: 25 g Sodium: 400 mg Carbohydrates: 20 g Protein: 10 g Fiber: 5 g

Tuna Quinoa Salad with Avocado

 15 Min 15 Min ✗ 4

Ingredients:

✦ 1/2 cup quinoa
✦ 1 can (5 oz) tuna in water, drained
✦ 1 avocado, diced
✦ 1 red bell pepper, diced
✦ 1 tomato, diced
✦ 1/2 red onion, finely chopped
✦ 1 tbsp fresh lemon juice
✦ 1 tbsp olive oil
✦ Salt and pepper to taste
✦ Fresh cilantro or parsley, for garnish

This refreshing Tuna Quinoa Salad is packed with protein and healthy fats, making it a nutritious and satisfying meal. The creamy avocado combined with fresh veggies and a light lemon dressing makes it perfect for a light lunch or dinner.

Directions:

✦ Rinse the quinoa thoroughly under running water and cook according to the package instructions until tender. Drain and allow to cool.
✦ In a large bowl, combine the cooked quinoa, drained tuna, diced avocado, red bell pepper, tomato, and red onion.
✦ Drizzle with lemon juice and olive oil, and gently toss to evenly coat the ingredients.
✦ Season with salt and pepper to taste. Serve the salad on plates and garnish with fresh cilantro or parsley. Enjoy immediately!

Nutritional Information per Serving - Calories: 400' Fat: 20 g Sodium: 550 mg Carbohydrates: 30 g Protein: 25 g Fiber: 8 g

Veggie Couscous with Roasted Chickpeas

 10 Min 20 Min ✗ 4

Ingredients:

✦ 1/2 cup couscous
✦ 1 small zucchini, diced
✦ 1 red bell pepper, diced
✦ 1 small carrot, thinly sliced
✦ 1/2 can (about 7 oz) chickpeas, drained and rinsed
✦ 1 tbsp olive oil
✦ 1 tsp ground cumin
✦ 1 tsp paprika
✦ Salt and pepper to taste
✦ Fresh parsley, for garnish

This vibrant salad pairs the earthy sweetness of roasted beets with creamy goat cheese and crunchy walnuts. A light balsamic dressing ties it all together, making it a perfect appetizer or light meal.

Directions:

✦ Prepare the couscous according to the package instructions and set aside.
✦ Preheat the oven to 400°F and line a baking sheet with parchment paper.
✦ Spread the drained chickpeas on the baking sheet, drizzle with 1 tsp olive oil, and season with cumin, paprika, salt, and pepper.
✦ Toss to coat evenly and roast in the oven for about 20 minutes until crispy.
✦ Meanwhile, heat 1 tbsp olive oil in a skillet over medium heat. Add the zucchini, red bell pepper, and carrot, sautéing for 5-7 minutes until the vegetables are tender.
✦ Mix the sautéed vegetables into the cooked couscous.
✦ Serve the couscous topped with the roasted chickpeas and garnish with fresh parsley.

Nutritional Information per Serving - Calories: 450 Fat: 15 g Sodium: 600 mg Carbohydrates: 35 g Protein: 20 g Fiber: 12 g

Roasted Chicken Thighs with Oven Vegetables

 15 Min 40 Min ✗ 4

A hearty and easy-to-make dish featuring tender roasted chicken thighs paired with golden roasted vegetables. This recipe makes for a comforting meal that's both healthy and satisfying.

Ingredients:

✧ 4 chicken thighs
✧ 4 small potatoes, diced
✧ 4 carrots, sliced
✧ 2 zucchinis, chopped
✧ 4 tbsp olive oil
✧ 1 tsp dried herbs (e.g. rosemary, thyme, oregano)
✧ Salt and pepper to taste
✧ Fresh parsley for garnish

Directions:

✧ Preheat the oven to 400°F.
✧ Wash and pat dry the chicken thighs, then season with salt, pepper, and dried herbs.
✧ In a baking dish, combine the diced potatoes, carrot slices, and chopped zucchini. Drizzle with olive oil, season with salt and pepper, and toss to coat evenly.
✧ Place the seasoned chicken thighs on top of the vegetables. Roast in the preheated oven for about 35-40 minutes until the chicken is fully cooked and the vegetables are golden and tender.
✧ Garnish with fresh parsley before serving.

Nutritional Information per Serving- Calories: 450' Fat: 20 g Sodium: 600 mg Carbohydrates: 35 g Protein: 25 g Fiber: 6 g

Vegetarian Chili Sin Carne with Black Beans

 10 Min 30 Min ✗ 4

A flavorful and hearty vegetarian chili made with black beans and spices. This plant-based dish is perfect for a cozy, satisfying meal and can be garnished with fresh herbs for added brightness.

Ingredients:

✧ 1 small onion, chopped
✧ 1 garlic clove, chopped
✧ 1 tbsp olive oil
✧ 1 tsp ground cumin
✧ 1 tsp paprika
✧ 1 tsp chili powder (adjust for desired heat)
✧ 1 can (14 oz) black beans, drained and rinsed
✧ 1 can (14 oz) diced tomatoes
✧ 1 red bell pepper, diced
✧ Salt and pepper to taste
✧ Fresh cilantro or parsley for garnish

Directions:

✧ In a large pot, heat the olive oil over medium heat.
✧ Add the chopped onion and garlic, sautéing until translucent.
✧ Stir in the ground cumin, paprika, and chili powder, cooking briefly until fragrant.
✧ Add the black beans, diced tomatoes, and red bell pepper to the pot, stirring well to combine.
✧ Bring the chili to a boil, then reduce the heat and let it simmer for 20-25 minutes until the bell pepper is tender and the sauce has thickened.
✧ Season with salt and pepper to taste. Garnish with fresh cilantro or parsley before serving.

Nutritional Information per Serving- Calories: 350 Fat: 8 g Sodium: 1000 mg Carbohydrates: 55 g Protein: 15 g Fiber: 15 g

Chapter 7

Sides and Salads for an Anti-Inflammatory Lifestyle

Eating to reduce inflammation doesn't have to be complicated or restrictive—it can be as simple as enjoying a delicious side dish or a vibrant salad. In this chapter, you'll discover a variety of side dishes and salads crafted to perfectly complement your meals while supporting your journey to a healthier, inflammation-free life. These nutrient-dense recipes are packed with fresh vegetables, whole grains, and healthy fats, all carefully selected for their ability to promote healing, boost immunity, and reduce inflammation in the body. Whether you're looking for a light and refreshing side or a heartier salad that could even double as a main, this collection offers a range of delicious, easy-to-make options that will leave you feeling nourished and energized. From crisp roasted vegetable medleys to zesty grain salads loaded with herbs, each recipe is designed to add variety and flavor to your diet. Embrace the power of food to soothe inflammation, enhance your well-being, and enjoy each bite as part of your ongoing wellness journey.

Mediterranean Quinoa Salad with Olives and Feta

 20 Min   15 Min    4

This light and refreshing Mediterranean quinoa salad is packed with flavor from fresh vegetables, briny olives, and creamy feta. It's a perfect side dish for any meal or a great standalone option for a healthy lunch.

Ingredients:

✧ 1 cup quinoa
✧ 1/2 red onion, finely chopped
✧ 1/2 cucumber, diced
✧ 1 1/4 cups cherry tomatoes, halved
✧ 3/4 cups g feta cheese, crumbled
✧ 32 black olives, pitted and chopped
✧ 4 tbsp fresh parsley, chopped
✧ 4 tbsp olive oil
✧ 4 tbsp lemon juice
✧ Salt and pepper to taste

Directions:

✧ Rinse the quinoa thoroughly under cold water to remove any bitterness.
✧ In a medium saucepan, bring 2 cups of water to a boil, then add the quinoa. Reduce heat, cover, and simmer for about 15 minutes until the quinoa is tender and water is absorbed.
✧ Transfer the cooked quinoa to a large mixing bowl and allow it to cool slightly.
✧ Add the chopped red onion, diced cucumber, halved cherry tomatoes, crumbled feta cheese, chopped olives, and fresh parsley to the quinoa.
✧ Drizzle the salad with olive oil and lemon juice, then toss everything together until well combined.
✧ Season with salt and pepper to taste.
✧ Chill in the refrigerator for a bit before serving or enjoy immediately.

Nutritional Information per Serving - Calories: 320 Fat: 15 g Sodium: 1100 mg Carbohydrates: 35 g Protein: 10 g Fiber: 6 g

Crunchy Arugula Walnut Salad with Pomegranate Seeds

 10 Min   5 Min    4

Ingredients:

✧ 5 cups arugula
✧ 1 cup walnuts
✧ Seeds from 1 pomegranate (about 1 cup)
✧ 4 tbsp olive oil
✧ 4 tbsp balsamic vinegar
✧ Salt and pepper to taste

This vibrant and fresh arugula salad gets a delicious crunch from toasted walnuts and a burst of sweetness from pomegranate seeds. It's the perfect side dish to add color and texture to your meal.

Directions:

✧ Roughly chop the walnuts and toast them in a dry skillet over medium heat for 3-5 minutes until fragrant and lightly browned. Set aside to cool.
✧ Rinse and dry the arugula, then arrange it on a serving platter. Sprinkle the pomegranate seeds evenly over the arugula.
✧ Drizzle the olive oil and balsamic vinegar over the salad.
✧ Scatter the toasted walnuts on top and season with salt and pepper to taste.
✧ Gently toss the salad to combine and serve immediately.

Nutritional Information per Serving - Calories: 280' Fat: 22 g Sodium: 165 mg Carbohydrates: 15 g Protein: 5 g Fiber: 4 g

Baked Sweet Potato Mash with Rosemary

 10 Min   30 Min    4

Ingredients:

✧ 1 large sweet potato
✧ 1 tbsp olive oil
✧ 1 tsp fresh rosemary, chopped
✧ Salt and pepper to taste

This baked sweet potato mash is flavored with fresh rosemary and olive oil, making it a delicious and nutritious side dish. Perfectly golden and crispy on top, it's sure to become a favorite at your table.

Directions:

✧ Preheat the oven to 400°F and line a baking sheet with parchment paper.
✧ Wash and peel the sweet potato, then cut it into small cubes.
✧ Boil the sweet potato cubes in a pot of water for 15-20 minutes until tender. Drain and transfer them to a bowl.
✧ Mash the sweet potatoes with a potato masher or fork until smooth.
✧ Stir in the olive oil and chopped rosemary, and season with salt and pepper to taste.
✧ Spread the mashed sweet potatoes evenly onto the prepared baking sheet.

Nutritional Information per Serving - Calories: 200 Fat: 7 g Sodium: 90 mg Carbohydrates: 35 g Protein: 2 g Fiber: 5 g

Broccoli Almond Salad with Cranberries

 15 Min 5 Min ✕ 4

Ingredients:

- ✧ 1 1/4 cups broccoli, cut into florets
- ✧ 2 tbsp almonds, chopped
- ✧ 2 tbsp dried cranberries
- ✧ 1 tbsp olive oil
- ✧ 1 tbsp balsamic vinegar
- ✧ Salt and pepper to taste

This vibrant Broccoli Almond Salad with Cranberries combines the crunch of roasted almonds with the sweetness of dried cranberries, making it a refreshing and nutrient-packed side dish. It's perfect for a light lunch or as an accompaniment to your main meal.

Directions:

- ✧ Wash the broccoli and cut it into small florets.
- ✧ Blanch the broccoli florets in boiling water for about 2-3 minutes until they are slightly tender but still crisp.
- ✧ Drain the broccoli and rinse under cold water to stop the cooking process. Let it drain well and set aside.
- ✧ In a dry pan, lightly toast the chopped almonds over medium heat until golden and fragrant. Remove from heat and allow to cool.
- ✧ In a small bowl, whisk together the olive oil and balsamic vinegar, seasoning with salt and pepper.
- ✧ In a serving bowl, combine the blanched broccoli, toasted almonds, and dried cranberries.
- ✧ Pour the dressing over the salad and gently toss until all ingredients are evenly coated. Serve immediately and enjoy!

Nutritional Information per Serving- Calories: 200' Fat: 14 g Sodium: 180 mg Carbohydrates: 16 g Protein: 5 g Fiber: 5 g

Avocado Cucumber Salad with Lime Dressing

 10 Min 0 Min ✕ 4

Ingredients:

- ✧ 1 ripe avocado
- ✧ 1/2 cucumber
- ✧ Juice of 1 lime
- ✧ 1 tbsp olive oil
- ✧ Salt and pepper to taste
- ✧ Fresh cilantro leaves for garnish (optional)

This light and refreshing Avocado Cucumber Salad is a perfect side dish for a healthy meal. The creamy avocado pairs beautifully with the crisp cucumber and tangy lime dressing, creating a delicious and nourishing salad.

Directions:

- ✧ Halve the avocado, remove the pit, and scoop out the flesh with a spoon.
- ✧ Slice or dice the avocado as desired.
- ✧ Wash, peel, and thinly slice the cucumber. In a bowl, combine the avocado and cucumber slices.
- ✧ Drizzle the lime juice and olive oil over the salad. Season with salt and pepper and gently toss until everything is evenly coated.
- ✧ Serve the Avocado Cucumber Salad on a plate and garnish with fresh cilantro if desired.
- ✧ Serve immediately.

Nutritional Information per Serving - Calories: 250 Fat: 22 g Sodium: 200 mg Carbohydrates: 15 g Protein: 3 g Fiber: 10 g

Roasted Cauliflower with Turmeric and Coriander

 5 Min   20 Min   ✕ 4

Ingredients:

- ✧ 1 small head of cauliflower
- ✧ 1 tbsp olive oil
- ✧ 1 tsp ground turmeric
- ✧ 1 tsp ground coriander
- ✧ Salt and pepper to taste
- ✧ Fresh parsley for garnish (optional)

This flavorful roasted cauliflower dish combines the warmth of turmeric and the earthiness of coriander for a healthy and vibrant side. It's simple to prepare and makes a perfect complement to any meal. Garnish with fresh parsley for added color and freshness.

Directions:

- ✧ Preheat the oven to 400°F and line a baking sheet with parchment paper.
- ✧ Wash and dry the cauliflower, then cut it into small florets.
- ✧ In a large bowl, toss the cauliflower florets with olive oil until evenly coated. Add ground turmeric, ground coriander, salt, and pepper, and toss again to ensure the spices are evenly distributed.
- ✧ Spread the seasoned cauliflower florets on the prepared baking sheet in a single layer.
- ✧ Roast in the preheated oven for about 20 minutes, or until golden brown and crispy.
- ✧ Remove from the oven, garnish with fresh parsley if desired, and serve immediately.

Nutritional Information per Serving - Calories: 150' Fat: 7 g Sodium: 90 mg Carbohydrates: 20 g Protein: 5 g Fiber: 7 g

Green Bean and Almond Salad with Balsamic Dressing

 10 Min   15 Min   ✕ 4

Ingredients:

- ✧ 10 oz fresh green beans, trimmed
- ✧ 1.5 oz almonds, sliced or chopped
- ✧ 2 tbsp olive oil
- ✧ 1 tbsp balsamic vinegar
- ✧ Salt and pepper to taste
- ✧ Fresh parsley or basil for garnish (optional)

This crunchy and refreshing green bean salad is complemented by toasted almonds and a tangy balsamic dressing. It's perfect as a light side dish or a healthy lunch option. Add your favorite fresh herbs for extra flavor.

Directions:

- ✧ Bring a pot of water to a boil and blanch the green beans for about 5 minutes until tender but still crisp.
- ✧ Drain the beans and rinse them under cold water to stop the cooking process.
- ✧ In a dry pan, lightly toast the almonds over medium heat until golden brown and fragrant. Set them aside to cool.
- ✧ In a small bowl, whisk together olive oil, balsamic vinegar, salt, and pepper.
- ✧ Combine the blanched green beans and toasted almonds in a serving bowl. Drizzle with the balsamic dressing and toss to coat evenly.
- ✧ Garnish with fresh parsley or basil if desired, and serve immediately.

Nutritional Information per Serving - Calories: 250 Fat: 21 g Sodium: 312 mg Carbohydrates: 12 g Protein: 5 g Fiber: 4 g

Roasted Pumpkin with Maple Syrup Glaze

Ingredients:

✧ 7 oz pumpkin (e.g., Hokkaido)
✧ 1 tbsp maple syrup
✧ 1 tbsp olive oil
✧ 1 tsp cinnamon
✧ Pinch of salt
✧ Fresh thyme or rosemary for garnish (optional)

 10 Min   25 Min 4

This roasted pumpkin recipe combines the natural sweetness of pumpkin with a hint of cinnamon and a delightful maple syrup glaze. It's perfect for fall and can be served as a side dish or even as a light dessert.

Directions:

✧ Preheat the oven to 400°F and line a baking sheet with parchment paper.
✧ Wash and halve the pumpkin, then scoop out the seeds. Cut the pumpkin into slices about 2 cm thick.
✧ In a bowl, toss the pumpkin slices with olive oil, maple syrup, cinnamon, and a pinch of salt until evenly coated.
✧ Arrange the slices on the prepared baking sheet and roast in the preheated oven for 20-25 minutes, until the pumpkin is tender and golden brown.
✧ Remove from the oven and transfer to a serving plate.
✧ Garnish with fresh thyme or rosemary if desired, and serve immediately.

Nutritional Information per Serving - Calories: 180'
Fat: 7 g Sodium: 40 mg Carbohydrates: 30 g
Protein: 2 g Fiber: 5 g

Tomato-Mozzarella Salad with Basil

Ingredients:

✧ 5.5 oz ripe tomatoes
✧ 3.5 oz mozzarella cheese
✧ A few fresh basil leaves
✧ 1 tbsp extra virgin olive oil
✧ 1 tbsp balsamic vinegar
✧ Salt and pepper to taste

 10 Min   0 Min 4

A fresh and simple classic, this Tomato-Mozzarella Salad with Basil is perfect as a light side dish or appetizer. The combination of juicy tomatoes, creamy mozzarella, and fragrant basil is elevated with a drizzle of olive oil and balsamic vinegar.

Directions:

✧ Slice the tomatoes and mozzarella into thin slices.
✧ Wash and pat dry the basil leaves.
✧ On a plate, alternate layers of tomato and mozzarella slices.
✧ Scatter the basil leaves over the top of the arranged slices.
✧ Drizzle with olive oil and balsamic vinegar, then season with salt and pepper.
✧ Serve immediately for the freshest flavor.

Nutritional Information per Serving - Calories: 320 Fat: 25 g
Sodium: 790 mg Carbohydrates: 10 g Protein: 15 g Fiber: 2 g

Oven-Roasted Brussels Sprouts with Honey-Mustard Glaze

 5 Min   20 Min   ✗ 4

Ingredients:

✧ 20 oz Brussels sprouts
✧ 4 tbsp olive oil
✧ 4 tbsp honey
✧ 4 tsp mustard
✧ Salt and pepper to taste

These oven-roasted Brussels sprouts with a sweet and tangy honey-mustard glaze make the perfect side dish for any meal. They're crispy, flavorful, and easy to prepare.

Directions:

✧ Preheat the oven to 400°F and line a baking sheet with parchment paper.
✧ Clean and dry the Brussels sprouts, then halve them.
✧ Place the Brussels sprouts on the baking sheet, drizzle with olive oil, and toss to coat evenly.
✧ Season with salt and pepper. Roast in the preheated oven for about 20 minutes, stirring halfway through, until golden brown and crispy.
✧ While the sprouts are roasting, mix honey and mustard in a small bowl.
✧ After roasting, drizzle the Brussels sprouts with the honey-mustard glaze and toss to combine.
✧ Serve immediately.

Nutritional Information per Serving - Calories: 180' Fat: 8 g Sodium: 685 mg Carbohydrates: 25 g Protein: 3 g Fiber: 6 g

Spinach Mango Salad with Ginger Dressing

 15 Min   0 Min   ✗ 4

Ingredients:

✧ 14 oz fresh spinach
✧ 1 ripe mango, peeled and cubed
✧ 4 tbsp chopped almonds
✧ 4 tsp freshly grated ginger
✧ 4 tbsp olive oil
✧ 4 tbsp apple cider vinegar
✧ 4 tsp honey
✧ Salt and pepper to taste

This refreshing Spinach Mango Salad with a zesty ginger dressing is a delightful combination of sweet and savory. It's perfect for a light lunch or a flavorful side dish.

Directions:

✧ Wash the fresh spinach thoroughly and pat it dry.
✧ Place the spinach in a large salad bowl.
✧ Peel, pit, and cube the mango, then add it to the spinach.
✧ Sprinkle the chopped almonds on top.
✧ In a small bowl, whisk together the grated ginger, olive oil, apple cider vinegar, honey, salt, and pepper to create the dressing.
✧ Drizzle the dressing over the salad and gently toss until everything is evenly coated.
✧ Serve immediately.

Nutritional Information per Serving- Calories: 220 Fat: 12 g Sodium: 602 mg Carbohydrates: 28 g Protein: 4 g Fiber: 2 g

Crispy Potato Wedges with Rosemary

 10 Min 30 Min  4

Ingredients:

- ✧ 4 medium potatoes
- ✧ 4 tbsp olive oil
- ✧ 4 tsp fresh rosemary, chopped
- ✧ Salt and pepper to taste

These crispy potato wedges with a hint of rosemary are a perfect side dish for any meal. They're simple to prepare, deliciously crunchy, and full of flavor.

Directions:

- ✧ Preheat the oven to 400°F and line a baking sheet with parchment paper.
- ✧ Wash and dry the potatoes thoroughly, then cut them lengthwise into wedges.
- ✧ In a large bowl, toss the potato wedges with olive oil, chopped rosemary, salt, and pepper until evenly coated.
- ✧ Spread the wedges out on the prepared baking sheet in a single layer, making sure they don't overlap.
- ✧ Bake for 25-30 minutes, turning them occasionally, until the wedges are golden brown and crispy.
- ✧ Remove from the oven and serve immediately.

Nutritional Information per Serving - Calories: 220' Fat: 7 g Sodium: 220 mg Carbohydrates: 36 g Protein: 3 g Fiber: 4 g

Fresh Berry Walnut Salad with Lemon Vinaigrette

 15 Min 0 Min  4

Ingredients:

- ✧ 1 1/2 cups mixed berries (such as strawberries, raspberries, blueberries)
- ✧ 3/4 cup walnut halves
- ✧ 4 handfuls mixed leafy greens
- ✧ 4 tbsp olive oil
- ✧ 4 tbsp fresh lemon juice
- ✧ 4 tsp honey

This fresh berry walnut salad is light, refreshing, and packed with antioxidants. The zesty lemon vinaigrette perfectly complements the sweetness of the berries and the crunch of toasted walnuts, making it a delightful side or starter.

Directions:

- ✧ Wash and gently dry the mixed berries, slicing any larger berries in half or quarters.
- ✧ Roughly chop the walnuts and toast them in a dry pan over medium heat for about 3-5 minutes, until fragrant. Remove from heat and let cool.
- ✧ Arrange the mixed greens on plates and scatter the berries on top.
- ✧ In a small bowl, whisk together the olive oil, lemon juice, honey, salt, and pepper until the honey is fully dissolved.
- ✧ Drizzle the lemon vinaigrette over the salad, then sprinkle the toasted walnuts on top.
- ✧ Gently toss the salad and serve immediately.

Nutritional Information per Serving - Calories: 250 Fat: 20 g Sodium: 60 mg Carbohydrates: 15 g Protein: 4 g Fiber: 5 g

Chapter 8

Desserts and Treats Without Inflammatory Triggers

Even when following an anti-inflammatory diet, you can still indulge your sweet tooth without compromising your health or wellness goals. This chapter offers a selection of dessert and treat recipes that are not only delicious but also mindful of ingredients that can trigger inflammation, such as refined sugars and processed fats. Instead, we've crafted recipes that feature natural sweeteners like honey and maple syrup, along with nutrient-dense ingredients like dark chocolate, nuts, and fresh fruits. These recipes incorporate anti-inflammatory superfoods like turmeric, berries, and cacao, allowing you to enjoy a guilt-free treat while nourishing your body. From creamy, dairy-free ice creams to rich, fruit-filled crumbles and satisfying energy bites, there's a treat for every occasion. These desserts are perfect for anyone looking to enjoy healthier alternatives without sacrificing flavor or pleasure. Indulge in these wholesome treats and discover how easy it can be to satisfy your cravings while staying on track with your wellness journey!

Mixed Berry Chia Pudding with Almonds

 5 Min*    0 Min   4

* Plus 4 hours chilling time

This delightful chia pudding is an easy and healthy treat packed with antioxidants and fiber from the berries, plus a satisfying crunch from the almonds. Perfect for breakfast, dessert, or a snack, it can be prepared the night before and enjoyed anytime.

Ingredients:

✧ 8 tbsp chia seeds
✧ 2 cups almond milk
✧ 1 cup mixed berries (e.g., strawberries, raspberries, blueberries)
✧ 4 tbsp sliced almonds
✧ Honey or maple syrup to taste

Directions:

✧ In a medium bowl, whisk together the chia seeds and almond milk until well combined.
✧ Cover the mixture and refrigerate for at least 4 hours, or overnight, until it thickens into a pudding-like consistency.
✧ Wash the berries and, if needed, cut them into smaller pieces.
✧ When ready to serve, divide the chia pudding into bowls or glasses, top with the mixed berries, and sprinkle with sliced almonds.
✧ Drizzle with honey or maple syrup if desired. Serve immediately and enjoy!

Nutritional Information per Serving - Calories: 250 Fat: 15 g Sodium: 9 mg Carbohydrates: 20 g Protein: 8 g Fiber: 12 g

Coconut Ginger Smoothie Bowl with Tropical Fruits

 10 Min 0 Min  4

Ingredients:

✧ 4 ripe bananas, cut into pieces and frozen
✧ 1 2/3 cups coconut milk
✧ 4 tsp freshly grated ginger
✧ 8 tbsp Greek yogurt
✧ 2 tsp honey or maple syrup (optional)
✧ 1 whole pineapple, cut into pieces
✧ 2 mangos, cut into pieces
✧ 4 kiwis, peeled and sliced
✧ 4 tbsp shredded coconut
✧ Fresh mint leaves for garnish (optional)

This refreshing smoothie bowl combines creamy coconut, a hint of ginger, and vibrant tropical fruits for a healthy, energizing breakfast or snack. It's quick to prepare and packed with flavors and textures.

Directions:

✧ In a blender, combine the frozen banana pieces, coconut milk, freshly grated ginger, Greek yogurt, and honey or maple syrup (if using).
✧ Blend until the mixture reaches a smooth and creamy consistency.
✧ Pour the smoothie mixture into bowls.
✧ Arrange the pineapple, mango, and kiwi pieces on top of the smoothie.
✧ Sprinkle with shredded coconut and garnish with fresh mint leaves if desired.
✧ Serve immediately and enjoy this tropical delight!

Nutritional Information per Serving - Calories: 350' Fat: 15 g Sodium: 50 mg Carbohydrates: 50 g Protein: 5 g Fiber: 8 g

Avocado Chocolate Mousse with Fresh Berries

 15 Min 0 Min  4

Ingredients:

✧ 4 ripe avocados
✧ 8 tbsp unsweetened cocoa powder
✧ 8 tbsp maple syrup or honey
✧ 2 tsp vanilla extract
✧ A pinch of salt
✧ Fresh berries (e.g., strawberries, raspberries, blueberries) for garnish

This rich and creamy avocado chocolate mousse is a healthier twist on a classic dessert. It's naturally sweetened and topped with vibrant fresh berries for a perfect finish.

Directions:

✧ Halve the avocados, remove the pits, and scoop the flesh into a blender.
✧ Add the cocoa powder, maple syrup or honey, vanilla extract, and a pinch of salt.
✧ Blend until smooth and creamy, scraping down the sides as needed to ensure everything is well combined.
✧ Divide the avocado chocolate mousse into bowls or glasses.
✧ Garnish with fresh berries and serve immediately for a delicious, guilt-free treat!

Nutritional Information per Serving - Calories: 300 Fat: 22 g Sodium: 6 mg Carbohydrates: 25 g Protein: 4 g Fiber: 10 g

Lemon Blueberry Oatmeal Muffins

 10 Min   20 Min   4

These refreshing lemon blueberry muffins are a wholesome treat made with oats and sweetened naturally. Perfect for breakfast or a snack, they're bursting with flavor and nutrition.

Directions:

✧ Preheat the oven to 350°F and line a muffin tin with paper liners.
✧ In a blender, pulse the oats until they become a fine flour.
✧ In a bowl, whisk the eggs lightly.
✧ Add honey, Greek yogurt, almond milk, and vanilla extract, mixing well.
✧ Stir in the oat flour, baking powder, salt, lemon juice, and zest until a smooth batter forms.
✧ Gently fold in the fresh blueberries. Spoon the batter evenly into the muffin cups.
✧ Bake for 20-25 minutes, or until golden brown and a toothpick inserted in the center comes out clean. Let the muffins cool before serving.

Ingredients:

✧ 4 medium potatoes
✧ 4 tbsp olive oil
✧ 4 tsp fresh rosemary, chopped
✧ Salt and pepper to taste

Nutritional Information per Serving - Calories: 250 Fat: 7 g Sodium: 500 mg Carbohydrates: 40 g Protein: 8 g Fiber: 5 g

Strawberry Banana Nice Cream with Roasted Nuts

 5 Min   5 Min   4

This creamy and refreshing strawberry banana nice cream is a healthier alternative to traditional ice cream. Topped with crunchy roasted nuts, it's the perfect guilt-free treat for a hot day.

Ingredients:

✧ 4 ripe bananas, sliced and frozen
✧ 2 3/4 cups fresh strawberries, halved
✧ 4 tbsp almond milk (or other plant-based milk of choice)
✧ A handful of mixed nuts (such as almonds, walnuts, cashews)
✧ A pinch of cinnamon (optional)
✧ Fresh mint for garnish (optional)

Directions:

✧ Place the frozen banana slices and halved strawberries into a blender or food processor.
✧ Add the almond milk and blend until smooth and creamy, adding more milk as needed to achieve the desired consistency.
✧ Transfer the nice cream into bowls.
✧ In a dry pan over medium heat, toast the mixed nuts until lightly browned and fragrant, stirring occasionally.
✧ Sprinkle the roasted nuts over the nice cream and garnish with a pinch of cinnamon and fresh mint, if desired.
✧ Serve immediately and enjoy!

Nutritional Information per Serving - Calories: 300 Fat: 18 g Sodium: 5 mg Carbohydrates: 30 g Protein: 6 g Fiber: 7 g

Green Tea Matcha Chia Pudding with Coconut Milk

 5 Min*   0 Min   4

* Plus 2 hours soaking time

Ingredients:

- ✧ 8 tbsp chia seeds
- ✧ 4 tsp matcha green tea powder
- ✧ 1 1/2 cups coconut milk
- ✧ 4 tsp maple syrup or honey (optional)
- ✧ Fresh berries or fruits of your choice for serving

This refreshing and creamy matcha chia pudding is the perfect way to start your day or enjoy as a healthy snack. The earthy flavors of matcha combine beautifully with the richness of coconut milk and the freshness of berries or fruits.

Directions:

- ✧ In a medium bowl, combine chia seeds and matcha powder.
- ✧ Add the coconut milk and stir thoroughly to ensure the chia seeds and matcha are evenly mixed.
- ✧ Sweeten with maple syrup or honey, if desired, and stir again. Cover the bowl and refrigerate for at least 2 hours or overnight until the mixture reaches a pudding-like consistency.
- ✧ When ready to serve, give the pudding a good stir and top with fresh berries or fruits.
- ✧ Enjoy immediately!

Nutritional Information per Serving - Calories: 300' Fat: 22 g Sodium: 11 mg Carbohydrates: 25 g Protein: 4 g Fiber: 10 g

Mango Coconut Popsicles with Toasted Coconut Flakes

 10 Min*   0 Min   4

* Plus 4 hours freezing time

Ingredients:

- ✧ 1 ripe mango
- ✧ 4 tbsp coconut milk
- ✧ 1 tbsp honey or maple syrup (optional)
- ✧ 2 tbsp toasted coconut flakes

These tropical mango coconut popsicles are a refreshing and creamy treat with a hint of sweetness. Perfect for a hot day or as a healthy dessert option, with the added crunch of toasted coconut flakes.

Directions:

- ✧ Peel the mango, remove the pit, and cut the flesh into cubes.
- ✧ Place the mango cubes, coconut milk, and optional honey or maple syrup into a blender and blend until smooth.
- ✧ Stir in the toasted coconut flakes.
- ✧ Pour the mango mixture evenly into popsicle molds and insert popsicle sticks.
- ✧ Freeze for at least 4 hours or overnight until fully set.
- ✧ Remove the popsicles from the molds and serve immediately.

Nutritional Information per Serving- Calories: 150 Fat: 7 g Sodium: 20 mg Carbohydrates: 24 g Protein: 1 g Fiber: 3 g

Raspberry Coconut Smoothie with Flaxseeds

 5 Min   0 Min ✗ 4

Ingredients:

✧ 1 cup frozen raspberries
✧ 2/3 cup coconut milk
✧ 1 tbsp flaxseeds
✧ 1 tsp honey or maple syrup (optional)
✧ Fresh mint leaves for garnish (optional)

This refreshing and creamy smoothie combines the tartness of raspberries with the richness of coconut milk, topped with the health benefits of flaxseeds. Perfect for a quick breakfast or a nourishing snack.

Directions:

✧ Place the frozen raspberries, coconut milk, flaxseeds, and optional honey or maple syrup into a blender.
✧ Blend on high speed until smooth and creamy.
✧ Pour the smoothie into a glass.
✧ Garnish with fresh mint leaves if desired, and serve immediately.

Nutritional Information per Serving - Calories: 250' Fat: 18 g Sodium: 5 mg Carbohydrates: 20 g Protein: 4 g Fiber: 10 g

Pear and Ginger Crumble with Oat Topping

 10 Min   30 Min ✗ 4

Ingredients:

✧ 1 ripe pear, peeled, cored, and sliced
✧ 1 tsp fresh ginger, finely chopped
✧ 1 tbsp brown sugar
✧ 1/2 tsp cinnamon
✧ 2 tbsp oats
✧ 1 tbsp flour
✧ 1 tbsp sugar
✧ 2 tbsp butter, cold and cut into small pieces
✧ A pinch of salt

This warm and cozy pear and ginger crumble features a spiced fruit filling and a crunchy oat topping. Perfect for a comforting dessert that balances sweetness with a touch of spice.

Directions:

✧ Preheat the oven to 350°F.
✧ Arrange the pear slices in a small baking dish and sprinkle with fresh ginger, brown sugar, and cinnamon.
✧ In a separate bowl, combine the oats, flour, brown sugar, cold butter, and a pinch of salt.
✧ Use your fingers to mix until the topping forms a crumbly texture.
✧ Spread the oat mixture evenly over the pears.
✧ Bake for about 25-30 minutes until the top is golden and crisp.
✧ Let the crumble cool slightly before serving warm.

Nutritional Information per Serving - Calories: 300 Fat: 12 g Sodium: 180 mg Carbohydrates: 50 g Protein: 3 g Fiber: 6 g

Pineapple Basil Sorbet with Mint

 10* Min 0 Min 4

*Plus 4 hours freezing time

This refreshing sorbet combines the tropical sweetness of pineapple with the bright flavors of basil and mint. A perfect light dessert for hot days or as a palate cleanser between meals.

Ingredients:

- ✧ 1 1/4 cups fresh pineapple, chopped
- ✧ 5-6 basil leaves
- ✧ 1 tbsp fresh mint leaves
- ✧ Juice of 1/2 lime
- ✧ 1 tbsp honey (optional)
- ✧ 4 tbsp water
- ✧ Fresh mint leaves and pineapple pieces for garnish

Directions:

- ✧ In a blender, combine the fresh pineapple pieces, basil leaves, mint leaves, lime juice, and water.
- ✧ Blend until smooth with no chunks remaining. If desired, add honey and blend briefly to incorporate.
- ✧ Pour the mixture into a shallow, freezer-safe container and spread evenly.
- ✧ Cover and freeze for at least 4 hours or overnight until solid. Before serving, allow the sorbet to soften slightly, then scoop into bowls.
- ✧ Garnish with fresh mint leaves and pineapple pieces.
- ✧ Serve immediately.

Nutritional Information per Serving - Calories: 120' Fat: 1 g Sodium: 3 mg Carbohydrates: 30 g Protein: 1 g Fiber: 3 g

Apple-Cinnamon Cake with Walnuts

 10 Min  20 Min 4

This warm and cozy apple-cinnamon cake with walnuts is the perfect treat for a snack or dessert. It's lightly sweetened and has a delicious crunch from the walnuts and oats.

Ingredients:

- ✧ 1 small apple, peeled and thinly sliced
- ✧ 1/4 cup rolled oats
- ✧ 1 tbsp chopped walnuts
- ✧ 1 tbsp whole wheat flour
- ✧ 1 tbsp maple syrup or honey
- ✧ 1 tsp cinnamon
- ✧ 1 tsp coconut oil (for greasing the pan)

Directions:

- ✧ Preheat the oven to 350°F and lightly grease a small baking dish with coconut oil.
- ✧ Arrange the apple slices on the bottom of the dish.
- ✧ In a separate bowl, mix the oats, chopped walnuts, whole wheat flour, maple syrup (or honey), and cinnamon together until combined.
- ✧ Evenly sprinkle the oat mixture over the apples and gently press it down.
- ✧ Bake for about 20 minutes until the top is golden brown and crisp.
- ✧ Let the cake cool slightly before serving.

Nutritional Information per Serving - Calories: 250 Fat: 10 g Sodium: 18 mg Carbohydrates: 35 g Protein: 5 g Fiber: 5 g

Peach-Almond Tart with Honey

 15 Min   30 Min   ✗ 4

This delightful peach-almond tart is lightly sweetened with honey and has a crispy almond crust that pairs beautifully with the soft, juicy peaches. It's a perfect summer dessert!

Ingredients:

✧ 1 small peach, pitted and thinly sliced
✧ 1/4 cup almond flour
✧ 1 tbsp chopped almonds
✧ 1 tbsp oat flour
✧ 1 tbsp honey
✧ 1 tsp coconut oil (for greasing the pan)

Directions:

✧ Preheat the oven to 350°F and lightly grease a small tart pan with coconut oil.
✧ In a bowl, combine the almond flour, oat flour, chopped almonds, and honey, mixing until a dough-like consistency forms.
✧ Press the mixture evenly into the greased tart pan, creating a crust with raised edges.
✧ Arrange the peach slices over the almond crust.
✧ Bake the tart for 25-30 minutes, or until the crust is golden brown and the peaches are tender.
✧ Remove from the oven and allow to cool slightly before serving.

Nutritional Information per Serving - Calories: 220' Fat: 12 g Sodium: 3 mg Carbohydrates: 25 g Protein: 4 g Fiber: 4 g

Orange-Pomegranate Salad with Mint

 10 Min   0 Min   ✗ 4

This refreshing Orange-Pomegranate Salad is a delightful combination of sweet and tangy flavors, perfect for a light snack or a side dish. The fresh mint adds a burst of freshness while the optional honey enhances the natural sweetness.

Ingredients:

✧ 1 orange
✧ 1/3 cup pomegranate seeds
✧ A few fresh mint leaves
✧ 1 tsp honey (optional)

Directions:

✧ Peel the orange and slice it into thin rounds.
✧ Arrange the orange slices on a plate and sprinkle the pomegranate seeds evenly over them.
✧ Finely chop the fresh mint leaves and scatter them on top of the salad.
✧ For an extra touch of sweetness, drizzle with a teaspoon of honey if desired.
✧ Serve immediately and enjoy the vibrant flavors.

Nutritional Information per Serving- Calories: 90 Fat: 0 g Sodium: 2 mg Carbohydrates: 22 g Protein: 1 g Fiber: 4 g

Kiwi-Ginger Yogurt Popsicles with Pistachios

 15 Min 30 Min  4

* plus freezing time

Ingredients:

✧ 1 ripe kiwi
✧ 3 tbsp Greek yogurt
✧ 1 tsp freshly grated ginger
✧ 1 tsp honey (optional)
✧ 1 tbsp chopped pistachios

These refreshing Kiwi-Ginger Yogurt Popsicles combine the tangy taste of kiwi with the zing of fresh ginger, and a touch of crunch from chopped pistachios. Perfect for a healthy frozen treat!

Directions:

✧ Peel the kiwi and chop it into small pieces.
✧ Place the kiwi in a blender and puree until smooth.
✧ Add the Greek yogurt and freshly grated ginger to the kiwi puree. If you prefer a sweeter popsicle, stir in honey.
✧ Fold in the chopped pistachios, then pour the mixture into popsicle molds.
✧ Freeze for at least 4 hours or overnight until solid.
✧ Carefully remove the popsicles from the molds and serve immediately.

Nutritional Information per Serving - Calories: 120' Fat: 5 g Sodium: 38 mg Carbohydrates: 15 g Protein: 3 g Fiber: 3 g

Pumpkin Pecan Bread with Maple Syrup

 15 Min 1 hour  4

Ingredients:

✧ 3 tbsp pumpkin puree
✧ 1/4 cups pecans, chopped
✧ 1/3 cup flour
✧ 1 tsp baking powder
✧ 1/2 tsp cinnamon
✧ 1 egg
✧ 1 tbsp maple syrup
✧ A pinch of salt

This moist and flavorful Pumpkin Pecan Bread is naturally sweetened with maple syrup and packed with warm autumn spices. It's perfect as a breakfast treat or afternoon snack!

Directions:

✧ Preheat the oven to 350°F and grease a small loaf pan.
✧ In a bowl, combine the pumpkin puree, egg, and maple syrup.
✧ In a separate bowl, mix the flour, baking powder, cinnamon, and a pinch of salt.
✧ Gradually add the dry ingredients to the pumpkin mixture, stirring until a smooth batter forms.
✧ Fold in the chopped pecans. Pour the batter into the prepared loaf pan and smooth the top.
✧ Bake for about 1 hour, or until the bread is golden brown and a toothpick inserted in the center comes out clean.
✧ Allow the bread to cool completely before slicing and serving.

Nutritional Information per Serving- Calories: 300 Fat: 15 g Sodium: 85 mg Carbohydrates: 35 g Protein: 8 g Fiber: 5 g

Chapter 9

Anti-Inflammatory Drinks for Vitality and Wellness

In this chapter, we dive into the power of anti-inflammatory drinks that not only quench your thirst but also promote vitality, balance, and long-term wellness. These beverages are more than just delicious—they're crafted with ingredients known for their healing properties, making it easy to support your body throughout the day. Whether you're starting your morning with an energizing smoothie packed with leafy greens and berries, enjoying a revitalizing midday tonic, or winding down in the evening with a soothing tea infused with ginger and turmeric, each drink is designed to help reduce inflammation, boost your immune system, and enhance your overall health.

These recipes are packed with natural ingredients like antioxidant-rich berries, calming herbs, and inflammation-fighting spices, creating drinks that are simple to make and incredibly nourishing. Perfect for anyone looking to embrace a healthier lifestyle without sacrificing taste, these beverages make it easy to experience the benefits of anti-inflammatory ingredients in every sip. Incorporate these drinks into your daily routine and discover how delicious supporting your well-being can be!

Energizing Green Tea Smoothies

 5 Min    5 Min*   4

*(for steeping the tea)

These refreshing and energizing green tea smoothies are packed with healthy fats, vitamins, and antioxidants. Perfect for a revitalizing start to your day or as a mid-afternoon boost.

Ingredients:

✧ 1 green tea bag
✧ 2/3 cup hot water
✧ 1 banana, peeled and chopped
✧ 1 handful fresh spinach
✧ 1/2 avocado, peeled and pitted
✧ Juice of 1/2 lime
✧ 1 teaspoon honey (optional)
✧ A few ice cubes (optional)

Directions:

✧ Steep the green tea bag in 2/3 cup of hot water for 3-5 minutes, then let it cool.
✧ In a blender, combine the banana, fresh spinach, avocado, lime juice, and honey (if using).
✧ Pour in the cooled green tea and blend until smooth and creamy.
✧ If desired, add a few ice cubes and blend again for a chilled smoothie.
✧ Pour into a glass, garnish if desired, and serve immediately!

Nutritional Information per Serving - Calories: 220 Fat: 11 g Sodium: 30 mg Carbohydrates: 30 g Protein: 8 g Fiber: 7 g

Anti-Inflammatory Turmeric Latte

 5 Min   5 Min    4

Ingredients:

- ❖ 3/4 cup almond milk
- ❖ 1 tsp turmeric powder
- ❖ 1/2 tsp ginger powder
- ❖ A pinch of black pepper
- ❖ A pinch of cinnamon
- ❖ 1 tsp coconut oil
- ❖ Honey or maple syrup to taste (optional)

This soothing and warm turmeric latte is packed with anti-inflammatory ingredients like turmeric, ginger, and cinnamon. It's a perfect calming drink to enjoy any time of the day.

Directions:

- ❖ Warm the almond milk in a small pot over medium heat.
- ❖ Stir in the turmeric powder, ginger powder, black pepper, and cinnamon, making sure the ingredients are well combined.
- ❖ Add the coconut oil and continue stirring until it has fully melted into the mixture.
- ❖ Remove from heat and pour the golden milk into a cup.
- ❖ Sweeten with honey or maple syrup to taste.
- ❖ Enjoy your comforting, anti-inflammatory turmeric latte while it's hot!

Nutritional Information per Serving - Calories: 50' Fat: 3 g Sodium: 10 mg Carbohydrates: 5 g Protein: 1 g Fiber: 1 g

Refreshing Ginger-Lemon Watermelon Juice

 10 Min   0 min   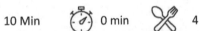 4

Ingredients:

- ❖ 1 1/4 cups watermelon, cubed
- ❖ Juice of 1/2 lemon
- ❖ 1 tsp fresh ginger, grated
- ❖ Ice cubes to taste
- ❖ A few mint leaves for garnish (optional)

This vibrant and refreshing watermelon juice with a zing of ginger and lemon is perfect for cooling down on a hot day. Garnish with fresh mint for an extra burst of flavor.

Directions:

- ❖ Place the cubed watermelon, lemon juice, and grated ginger into a blender.
- ❖ Blend until smooth.
- ❖ Strain the juice through a fine sieve to remove any pulp.
- ❖ Fill a glass with ice cubes and pour the strained juice over the top.
- ❖ Garnish with mint leaves if desired.
- ❖ Stir well and serve immediately for a cooling and revitalizing drink.

Nutritional Information per Serving - Calories: 80 Fat: 1 g Sodium: 3 mg Carbohydrates: 20 g Protein: 1 g Fiber: 1 g

Warming Cinnamon Apple Tea

 5 Min 10 Min ✕ 4

Ingredients:

✧ 1 apple, thinly sliced
✧ 1 cinnamon stick
✧ 1 cup water
✧ Honey to taste
✧ A few cloves (optional)

This cozy cinnamon apple tea is the perfect way to enjoy a comforting and fragrant drink during cooler days. Add a touch of honey for sweetness and cloves for extra spice.

Directions:

✧ Bring the water to a boil in a small pot.
✧ Add the apple slices, cinnamon stick, and cloves (if using) to the boiling water.
✧ Reduce the heat and let the mixture simmer for about 10 minutes to release the flavors.
✧ Remove from heat and strain the tea through a fine sieve or tea filter into a cup.
✧ Sweeten with honey as desired and serve warm.

Nutritional Information per Serving - Calories: 50' Fat: 0 g Sodium: 3 mg Carbohydrates: 13 g Protein: 0 g Fiber: 2 g

Revitalizing Beet Ginger Smoothies

 5 Min 0 min ✕ 4

This vibrant and refreshing beet ginger smoothie is packed with antioxidants and nutrients. It's a great way to boost your energy and vitality, perfect for starting the day or as a healthy snack.

Ingredients:

✧ 1 small cooked beet, chopped
✧ 1 small banana, peeled and chopped
✧ 1 teaspoon fresh ginger, peeled and finely chopped
✧ 2/3 cup almond milk
✧ Juice of 1/2 lemon
✧ 1 teaspoon honey (optional)
✧ A few ice cubes (optional)

Directions:

✧ Place all ingredients in a blender and blend on high speed until smooth and creamy.
✧ Adjust the consistency by adding more almond milk if needed.
✧ Pour the smoothie into a glass and serve immediately.

Nutritional Information per Serving - Calories: 150 Fat: 1 g Sodium: 60 mg Carbohydrates: 35 g Protein: 2 g Fiber: 6 g

Soothing Chamomile Lavender Tea

 5 Min   0 Min   ✗ 4

Ingredients:

◇ 1 chamomile tea bag or 1 teaspoon dried chamomile flowers
◇ 1 teaspoon dried lavender
◇ Honey or agave syrup to taste (optional)
◇ 1 cup boiling water

This calming chamomile lavender tea is the perfect way to unwind and relax, especially before bedtime. A touch of honey adds a hint of sweetness to this floral blend.

Directions:

◇ Bring water to a boil in a kettle.
◇ Place the chamomile tea bag or dried chamomile flowers and lavender into a teapot.
◇ Pour the boiling water over the herbs and let steep for about 5 minutes to allow the flavors to infuse.
◇ Sweeten with honey or agave syrup if desired.
◇ Strain the tea into a cup and serve hot.

Nutritional Information per Serving - Calories: 0' Fat: 0 g Sodium: 0 mg Carbohydrates: 0 g Protein: 0 g Fiber: 0 g

Antioxidant Berry-Avocado Smoothie

 5 Min   0 Min   ✗ 4

Ingredients:

◇ 2 3/4 cups mixed berries (e.g., raspberries, blackberries, blueberries)
◇ 2 ripe avocados
◇ 2 1/2 cups unsweetened almond milk
◇ 4 tbsp honey or maple syrup (optional)
◇ Juice of 2 lemons
◇ Fresh mint leaves (optional)
◇ Ice cubes (optional)

This creamy smoothie combines antioxidant-rich berries and healthy fats from avocado for a delicious and refreshing drink. Perfect for breakfast or as a revitalizing snack.

Directions:

◇ Add the mixed berries, avocados, almond milk, lemon juice, and honey or maple syrup (if using) to a blender.
◇ Optionally, add a few fresh mint leaves for extra flavor.
◇ Blend until smooth and creamy.
◇ If desired, add ice cubes and blend again to chill the smoothie.
◇ Pour into glasses, garnish with fresh berries or mint leaves, and serve immediately.

Nutritional Information per Serving - Calories: 220 Fat: 3 g Sodium: 21 mg Carbohydrates: 20 g Protein: 14 g Fiber: 7 g

Detoxifying Celery-Cucumber Juice

 5 Min   0 Min   ✕ 4

Ingredients:

- ✧ 2 cucumbers
- ✧ 8 celery stalks
- ✧ 4 green apples
- ✧ Juice of 2 lemons
- ✧ A handful of fresh parsley
- ✧ A pinch of sea salt
- ✧ Ice cubes (optional)

This refreshing and detoxifying juice is packed with hydrating cucumber, cleansing celery, and a touch of lemon for a zesty boost. Perfect for a revitalizing start to your day.

Directions:

- ✧ Wash the cucumbers, celery stalks, and green apples thoroughly, then cut them into pieces to fit into the juicer.
- ✧ Squeeze the lemon juice and add it to the juicer along with the fresh parsley.
- ✧ Process everything in a juicer until a smooth juice forms.
- ✧ Stir in a pinch of sea salt and, if desired, add ice cubes to chill.
- ✧ Pour the juice into glasses and serve immediately.

Nutritional Information per Serving - Calories: 70' Fat: 1 g Sodium: 195 mg Carbohydrates: 17 g Protein: 2 g Fiber: 3 g

Energizing Matcha Lemonade

 5 Min   0 Min   ✕ 4

Ingredients:

- ✧ 4 teaspoons matcha powder
- ✧ 4 cups water
- ✧ Juice of 2 lemons
- ✧ 4 teaspoons honey or agave syrup
- ✧ Ice cubes
- ✧ Fresh mint leaves for garnish (optional)

This refreshing Matcha Lemonade is the perfect pick-me-up with a blend of earthy matcha and tangy lemon. It's great as a cooling beverage with a boost of antioxidants.

Directions:

- ✧ Place the matcha powder in a cup.
- ✧ Add a small amount of hot water and whisk until smooth, avoiding clumps.
- ✧ Add the rest of the water and mix well.
- ✧ Stir in the freshly squeezed lemon juice and sweeten to taste with honey or agave syrup.
- ✧ Fill a glass with ice cubes, pour the matcha lemonade over the ice, and garnish with fresh mint leaves if desired.
- ✧ Stir well and serve immediately.

Nutritional Information per Serving - Calories: 20 Fat: 1 g Sodium: 1 mg Carbohydrates: 5 g Protein: 1 g Fiber: 1 g

Anti-Inflammatory Blueberry Chia Smoothies

 5 Min   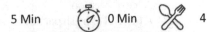 0 Min   ✗ 4

Ingredients:

✧ 1 1/3 cups blueberries (fresh or frozen)
✧ 1 ripe banana
✧ 4 tablespoons chia seeds
✧ 2/3 cup almond milk (or any plant-based milk)
✧ 4 teaspoons honey or maple syrup (optional)
✧ Ice cubes (optional)

This delicious and nutritious smoothie combines antioxidant-rich blueberries and chia seeds for a healthy, anti-inflammatory boost. Perfect for breakfast or a refreshing snack.

Directions:

✧ Add the blueberries to a blender.
✧ Peel and slice the banana, then add it to the blender.
✧ Add the chia seeds and almond milk. If desired, sweeten with honey or maple syrup.
✧ Optionally, add some ice cubes to make the smoothie cooler and more refreshing.
✧ Blend everything until smooth. Pour into glasses and serve immediately.

Nutritional Information per Serving - Calories: 250' Fat: 4 g Sodium: 10 mg Carbohydrates: 50 g Protein: 5 g Fiber:1 0 g

Invigorating Mint-Orange Juice

 5 Min    0 Min   ✗ 4

Ingredients:

✧ 8 large oranges
✧ A few fresh mint leaves
✧ Ice cubes (optional)
✧ Honey or agave syrup to taste (optional)

This refreshing juice combines the zesty taste of oranges with the cooling essence of mint. Perfect for a quick energy boost or as a revitalizing drink on a hot day.

Directions:

✧ Juice the oranges to extract fresh orange juice and pour it into a glass.
✧ Wash and pat dry the mint leaves.
✧ Rub a few mint leaves between your palms to release their aroma and add them to the orange juice.
✧ If desired, sweeten with honey or agave syrup.
✧ Optionally, add a few ice cubes to chill the juice.
✧ Stir well to mix the flavors and serve immediately.

Nutritional Information per Serving - Calories: 100 Fat: 0 g Sodium: 2 mg Carbohydrates: 25 g Protein: 2 g Fiber: 3 g

Strengthening Turmeric-Ginger Tea

 5 Min   5 Min   ✗ 4

This warm and invigorating tea combines the anti-inflammatory properties of turmeric and ginger with the zesty freshness of lemon. Perfect for boosting your immune system and promoting overall wellness.

Ingredients:

✧ 4 teaspoons fresh grated ginger
✧ 4 teaspoons fresh grated turmeric (or 2 teaspoons ground turmeric)
✧ 4 cups water
✧ A splash of freshly squeezed lemon juice
✧ Honey or maple syrup to taste (optional)

Directions:

✧ Bring water to a boil in a small pot.
✧ Add the fresh ginger and turmeric, then simmer for 3-5 minutes to release their flavors.
✧ Strain the tea through a fine sieve into a cup to remove the ginger and turmeric pieces.
✧ Add a splash of freshly squeezed lemon juice, and if desired, sweeten with honey or maple syrup.
✧ Stir well and serve warm.

Nutritional Information per Serving - Calories: 10' Fat: 0 g Sodium: 2 mg Carbohydrates: 2 g Protein: 0 g Fiber:1 g

Refreshing Cucumber-Mint Smoothies

 5 Min   0 Min   ✗ 4

This light and cooling smoothie is perfect for hot days. It combines the refreshing taste of cucumber and mint with the creaminess of Greek yogurt, creating a balanced and hydrating drink.

Ingredients:

✧ 2 cucumbers, peeled and chopped
✧ 1 handful of fresh mint leaves
✧ 2 bananas, peeled
✧ 2 cups Greek yogurt
✧ Juice of 1 lime
✧ Ice cubes (optional)

Directions:

✧ Place all ingredients in a blender and blend until smooth and creamy.
✧ If desired, add ice cubes and blend again to chill the smoothie.
✧ Pour into glasses and serve immediately.

Nutritional Information per Serving - Calories: 120 Fat: 1 g Sodium: 30 mg Carbohydrates: 20 g Protein: 7 g Fiber: 5 g

Soothing Lavender Honey Tea

 5 Min   0 Min   ✗ 4

Ingredients:

✧ 4 teaspoons dried lavender flowers
✧ 4 cups water
✧ 4 teaspoons honey (optional)

This calming tea is perfect for relaxing moments, with the gentle floral notes of lavender. Add a touch of honey for extra sweetness, if desired.

Directions:

✧ Bring the water to a boil in a small pot.
✧ Place the lavender flowers in a tea filter or tea infuser and put it in a cup.
✧ Pour the boiling water over the lavender and let the tea steep for 5-7 minutes to release the flavors.
✧ Sweeten with honey if desired, stir, and remove the lavender before serving.

Nutritional Information per Serving - Calories: 0' Fat: 0 g Sodium: 1 mg Carbohydrates: 0 g Protein: 0 g Fiber: 0 g

Revitalizing Pineapple Coconut Water Smoothie

 5 Min   0 Min   ✗ 4

Ingredients:

✧ 2 cups pineapple chunks, fresh or frozen
✧ 2 cups coconut water
✧ 1 cup Greek yogurt
✧ 4 teaspoons honey (optional)
✧ A few ice cubes (optional)

This refreshing smoothie combines the tropical flavors of pineapple and coconut water for a hydrating and energizing drink. Add a touch of honey for extra sweetness if desired.

Directions:

✧ Place the pineapple chunks, coconut water, Greek yogurt, and honey (if using) into a blender.
✧ Blend until smooth and creamy.
✧ Add a few ice cubes and blend again if you prefer a colder, thicker smoothie.
✧ Pour into glasses and serve immediately.

Nutritional Information per Serving- Calories: 120 Fat: 0 g Sodium: 71 mg Carbohydrates: 25 g Protein: 3 g Fiber: 2 g

Conclusion

The conclusion of a book is an opportunity to bring together the key themes, draw final thoughts, and leave the reader with a lasting message. In this chapter, I'd like to reflect on the essence of our journey through the world of anti-inflammatory eating and healthy living.

Together, we've explored an abundance of information that has shown us how a diet rich in anti-inflammatory foods can not only improve our health but also enhance our overall sense of well-being. From delicious main dishes free of inflammation-triggering ingredients to refreshing beverages that support our vitality, we've discovered a variety of recipes and ideas that can help reduce inflammation in the body while still being enjoyable and nourishing.

It's essential to remember that adopting an anti-inflammatory diet is not a rigid set of rules, but rather a lifestyle that can be tailored to meet individual needs. Every body is unique, and what works well for one person may not necessarily work for another. That's why it's so important to listen to your body and make adjustments to your diet based on your own experience and well-being.

In addition to dietary choices, we've also considered the significant role of movement, stress management, and maintaining a balanced lifestyle in reducing inflammation. Taking a holistic approach to our health is crucial— nutrition is just one piece of the larger puzzle of self-care. Incorporating mindful practices like exercise, rest, and stress reduction alongside a nutritious diet forms a powerful foundation for reducing inflammation and promoting lasting health.

As we close this chapter, I want to encourage you to apply the knowledge and inspiration you've gained from this book to your everyday life. Even small changes can make a big impact. Be mindful of your body, choose foods that energize and revitalize you, and enjoy the journey toward a healthier, inflammation-free life.

May this book inspire you to find your own path toward a life filled with health, happiness, and well-being. Thank you for taking this journey with me.

Megan

Bonus Content

Dear readers,

I am very pleased to present you with our bonus material *The 5 Secrets to a Life Without Inflammation*. As a thank you for your support and interest in this book, I would like to give you some exclusive tips that can help you reduce inflammation and increase your well-being.

In this bonus you will find five valuable strategies that you can easily integrate into your everyday life. From dietary recommendations to effective ways to manage stress, these secrets will provide you with practical tools for a healthier life.

A special thank you to all those who have followed the path we have taken together to get here. Your willingness to engage with the contents of this book deserves recognition.

To access this bonus, simply scan the QR code that you will find immediately after this text. I hope that this additional information will provide you with new inspiration and motivation.

Thank you for your trust and enjoy discovering the secrets!

Kind regards,

Megan

Made in the USA
Las Vegas, NV
23 November 2024

12418771R10044